**MANDALA COLORING PENCIL BOOK FOR ADULT AND TEEN**

**BEST FOR**

# RELAXATION. INSPIRATION.
## STRESS RELIEVING AND MEDITATION.

"THE BEST COLOR IN THE WHOLE WORLD,
IS THE ONE THAT LOOKS GOOD ON YOU."

Copyright © 2021 by Sophia Color
All rights reserved. This book or any portion thereof
may not be reproduced or used in any manner whatsoever
without the express written permission of the publisher
except for the use of brief quotations in a book review.

First Printing, 2021

ISBN 9798561516603

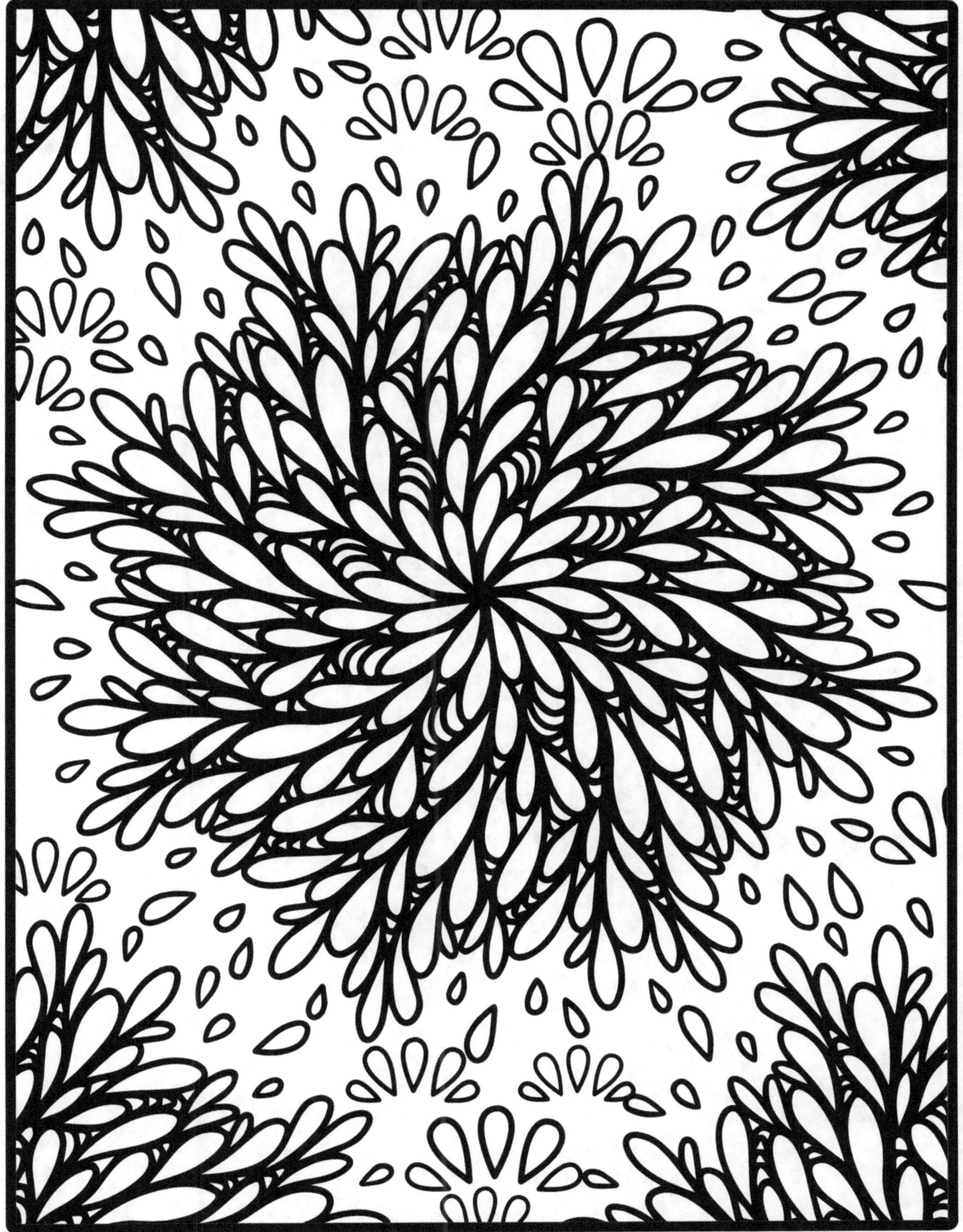

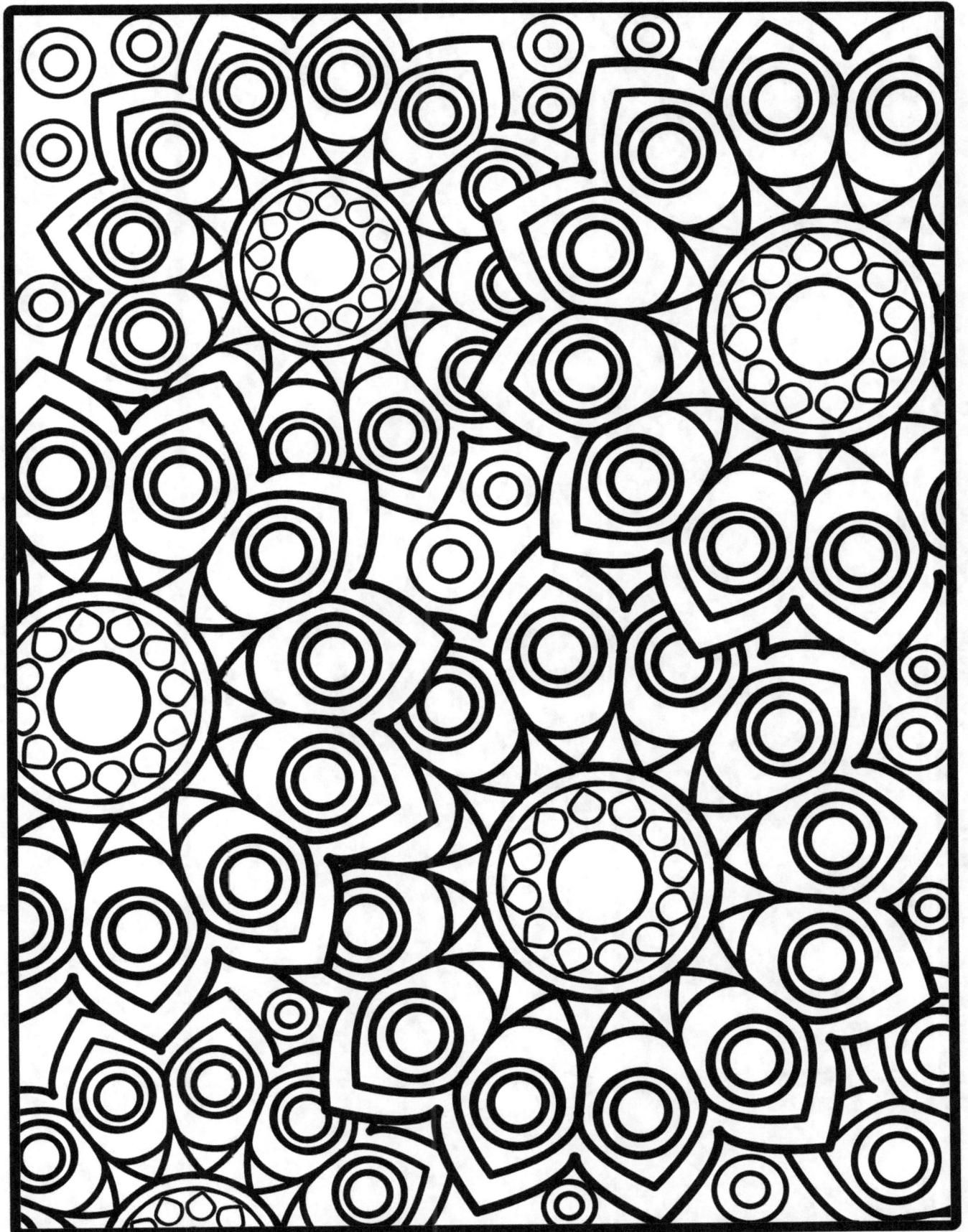

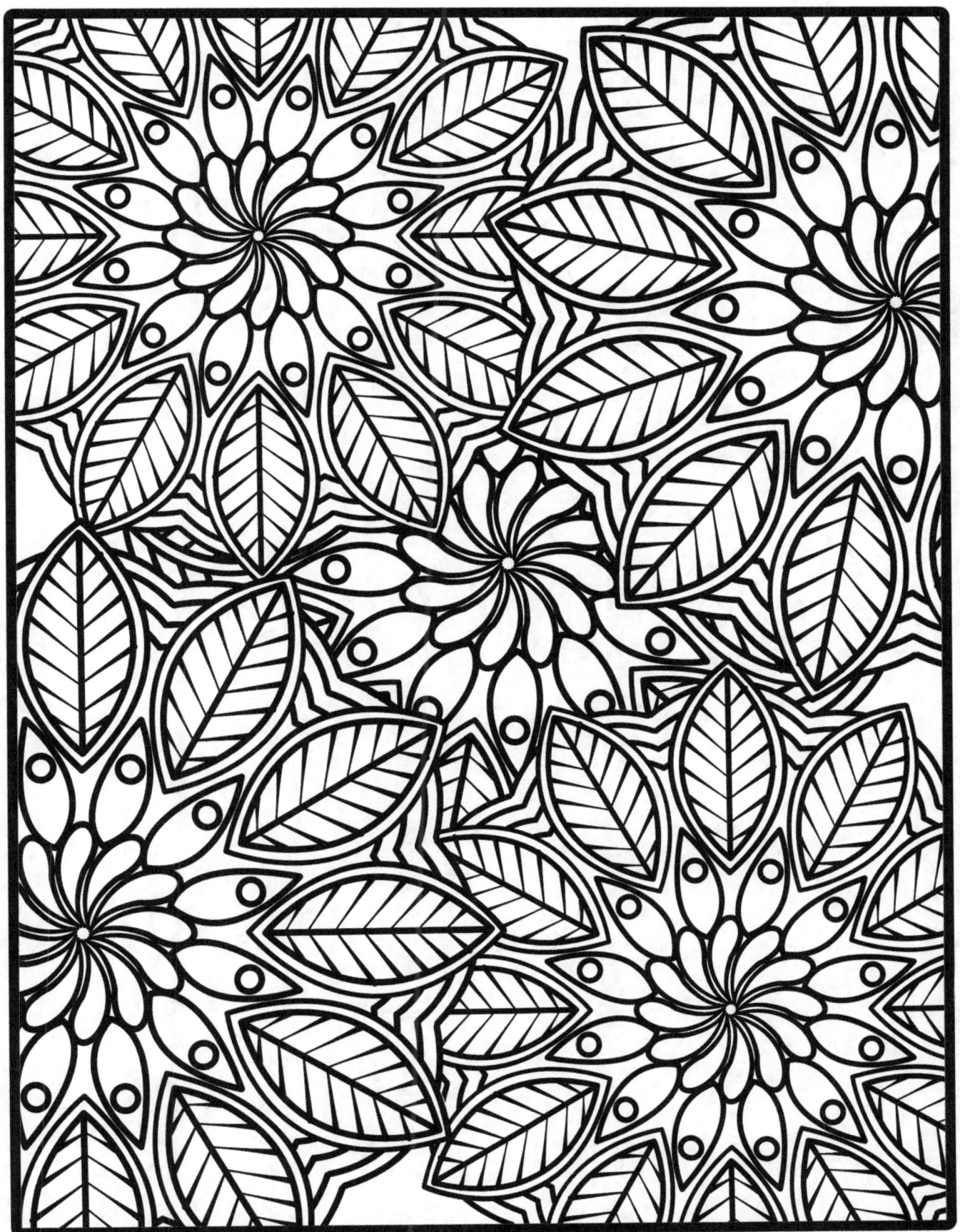

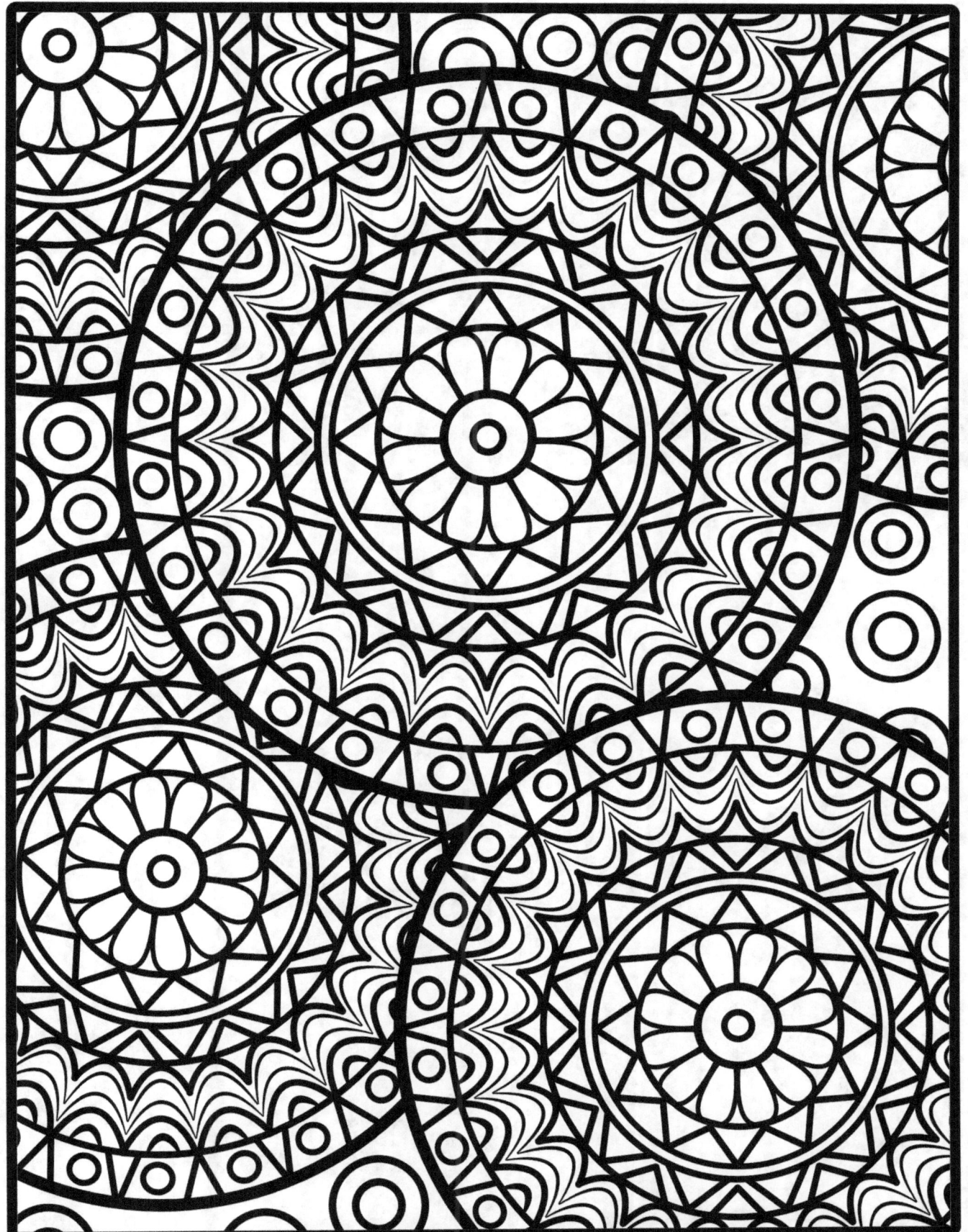

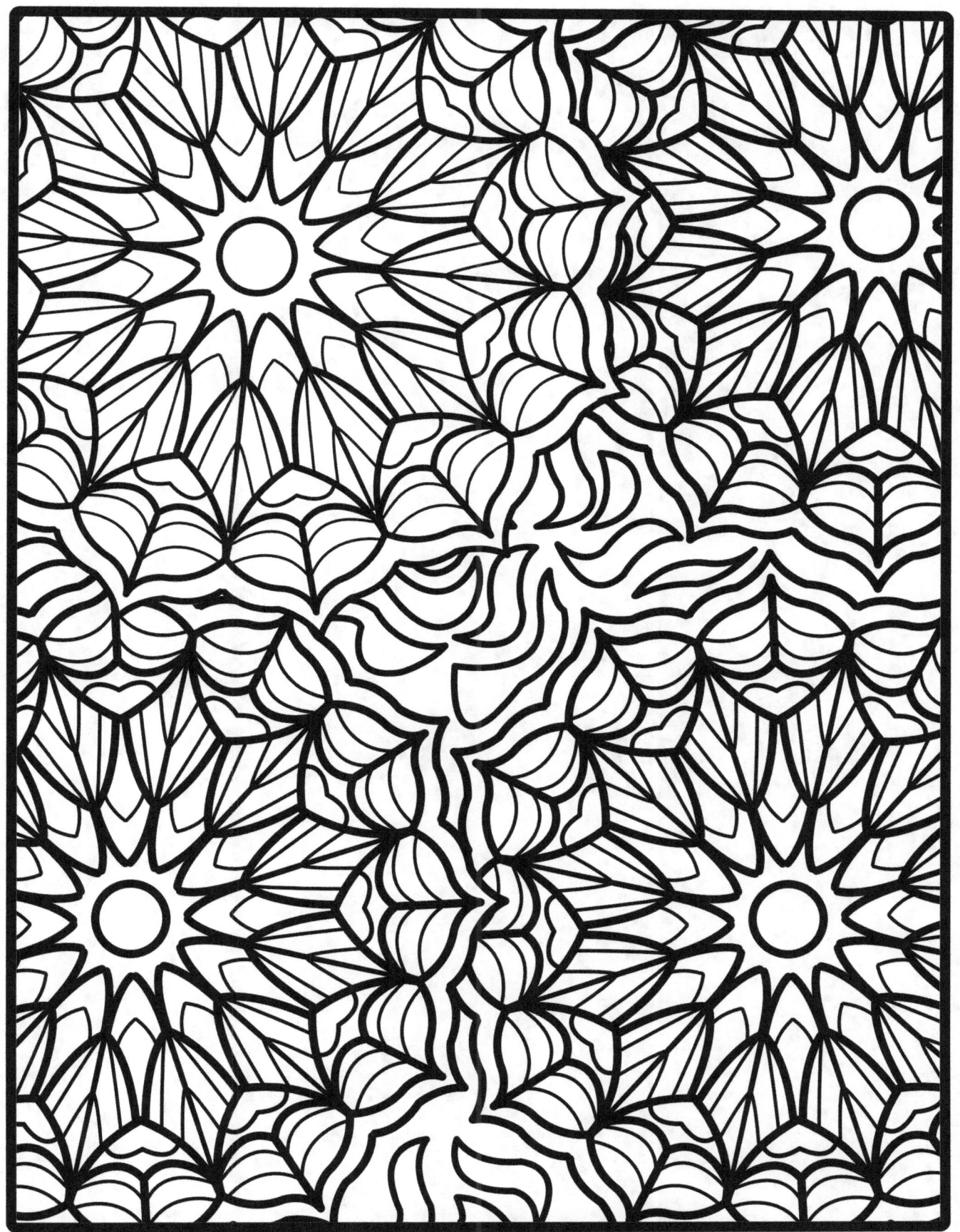

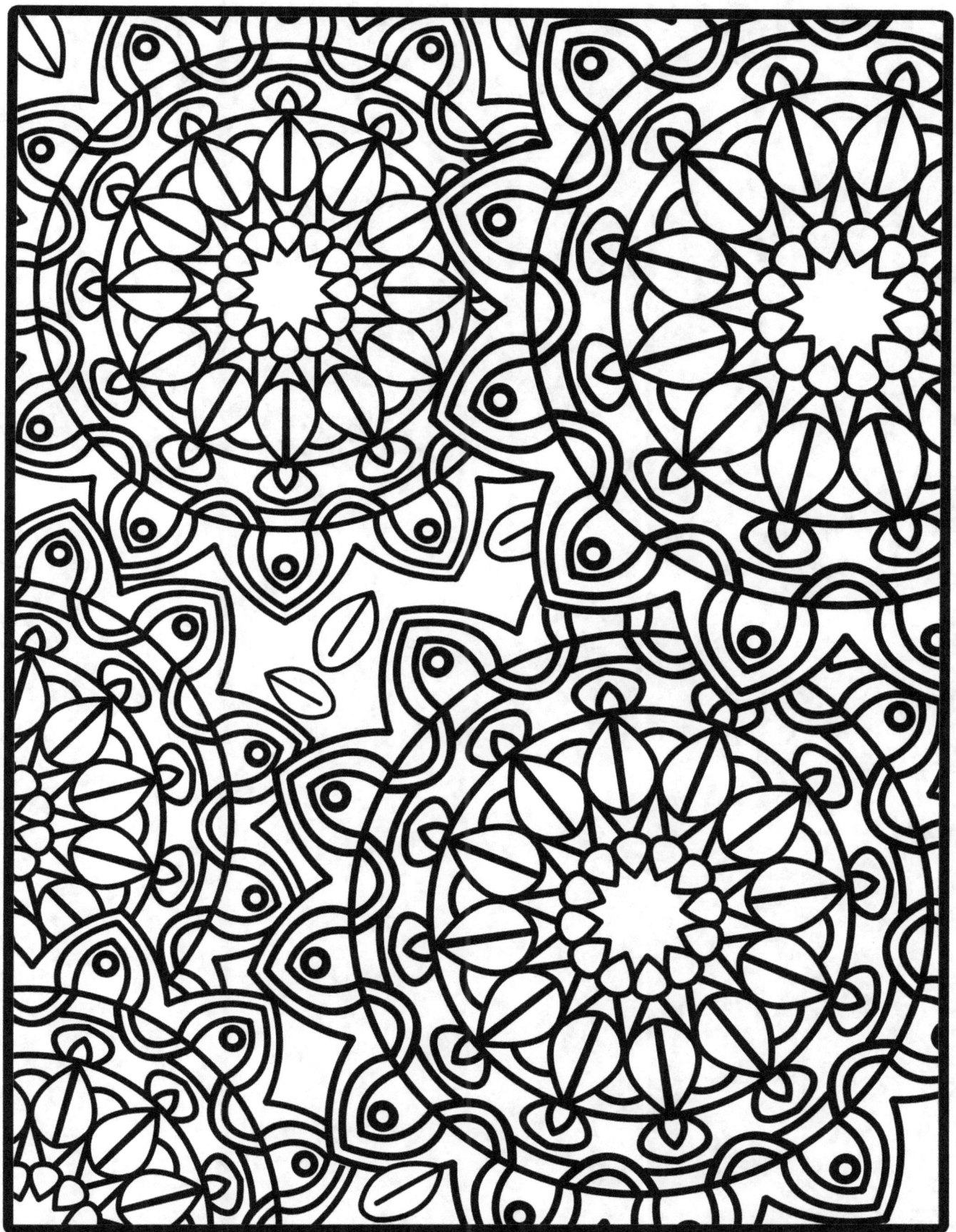

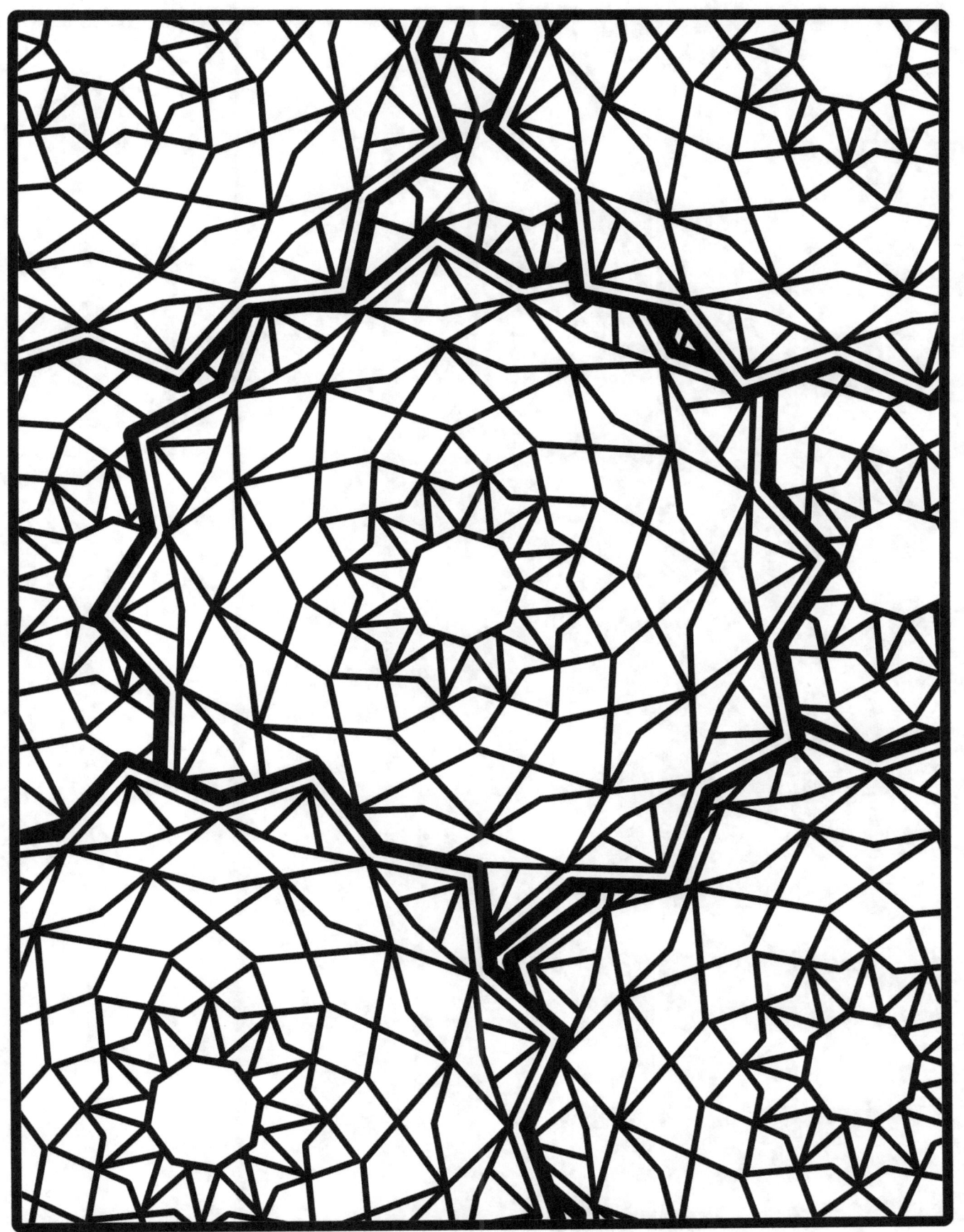

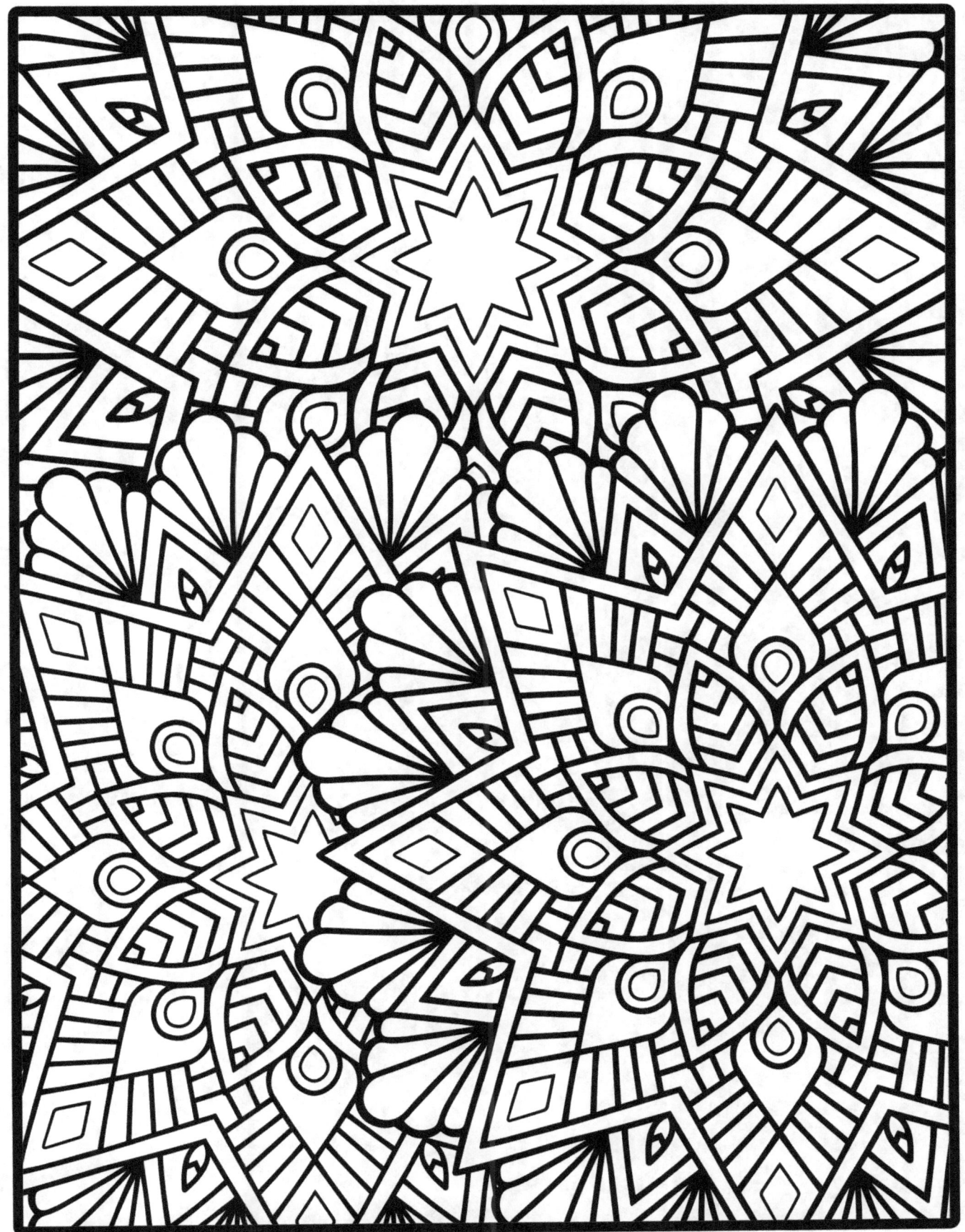

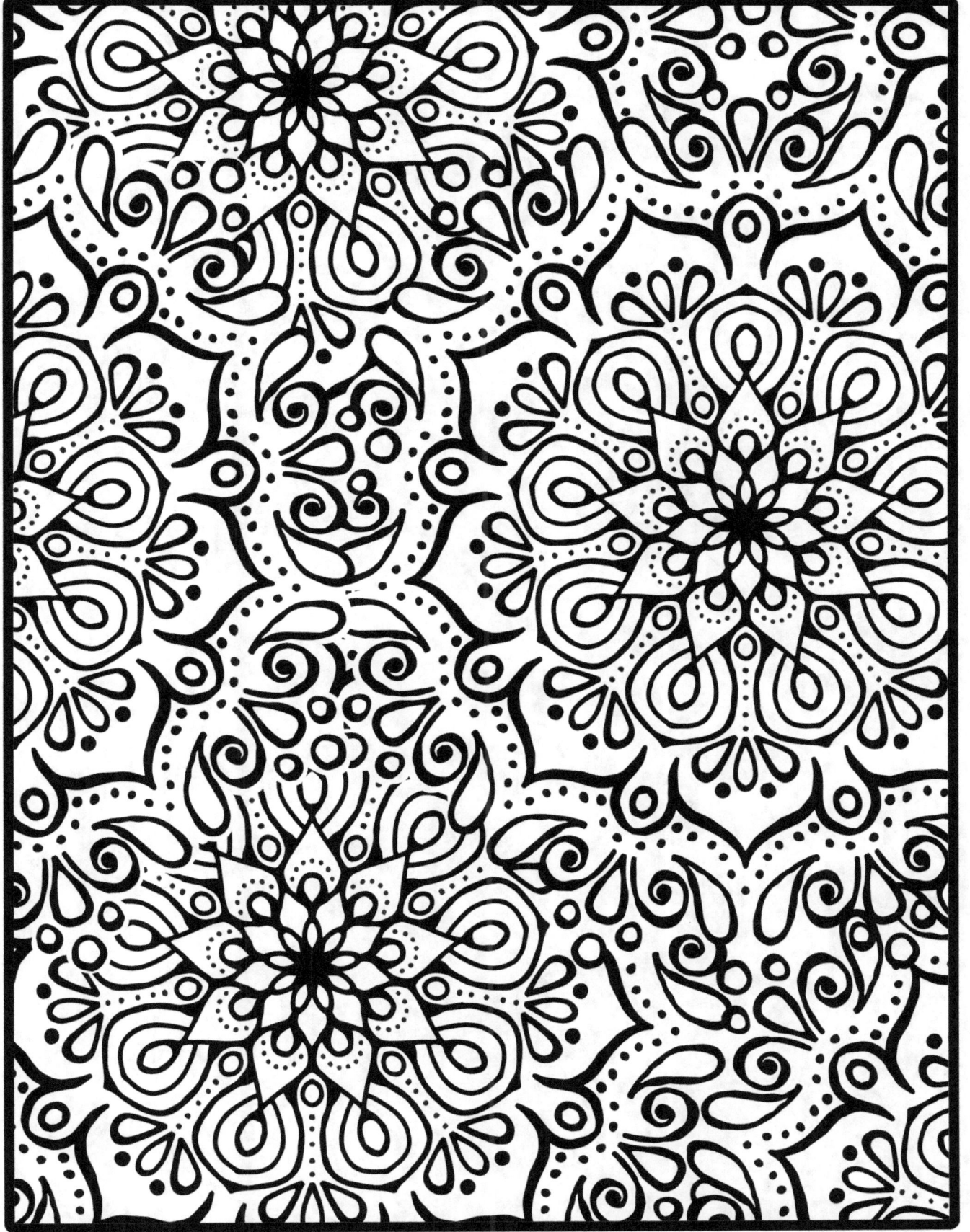

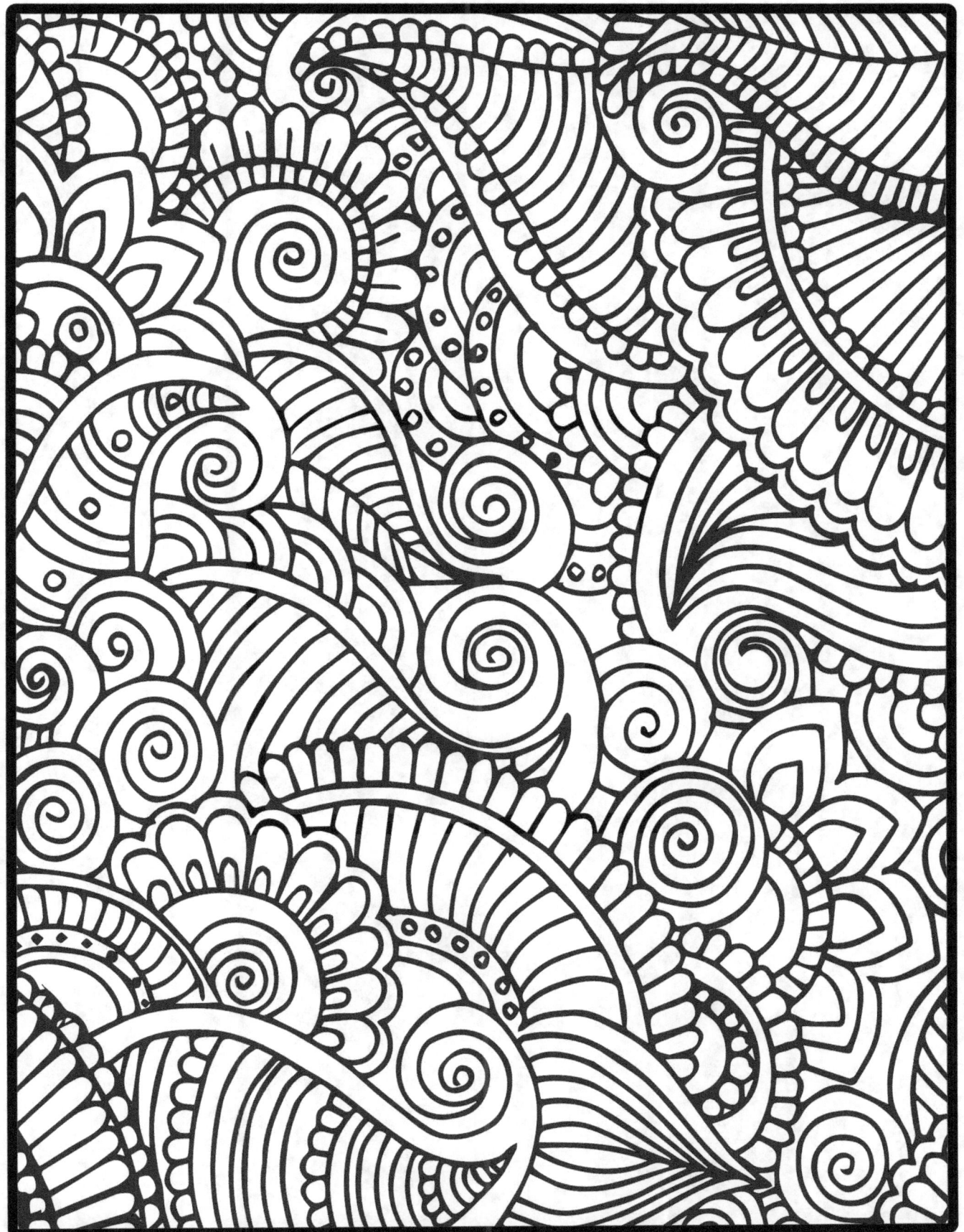

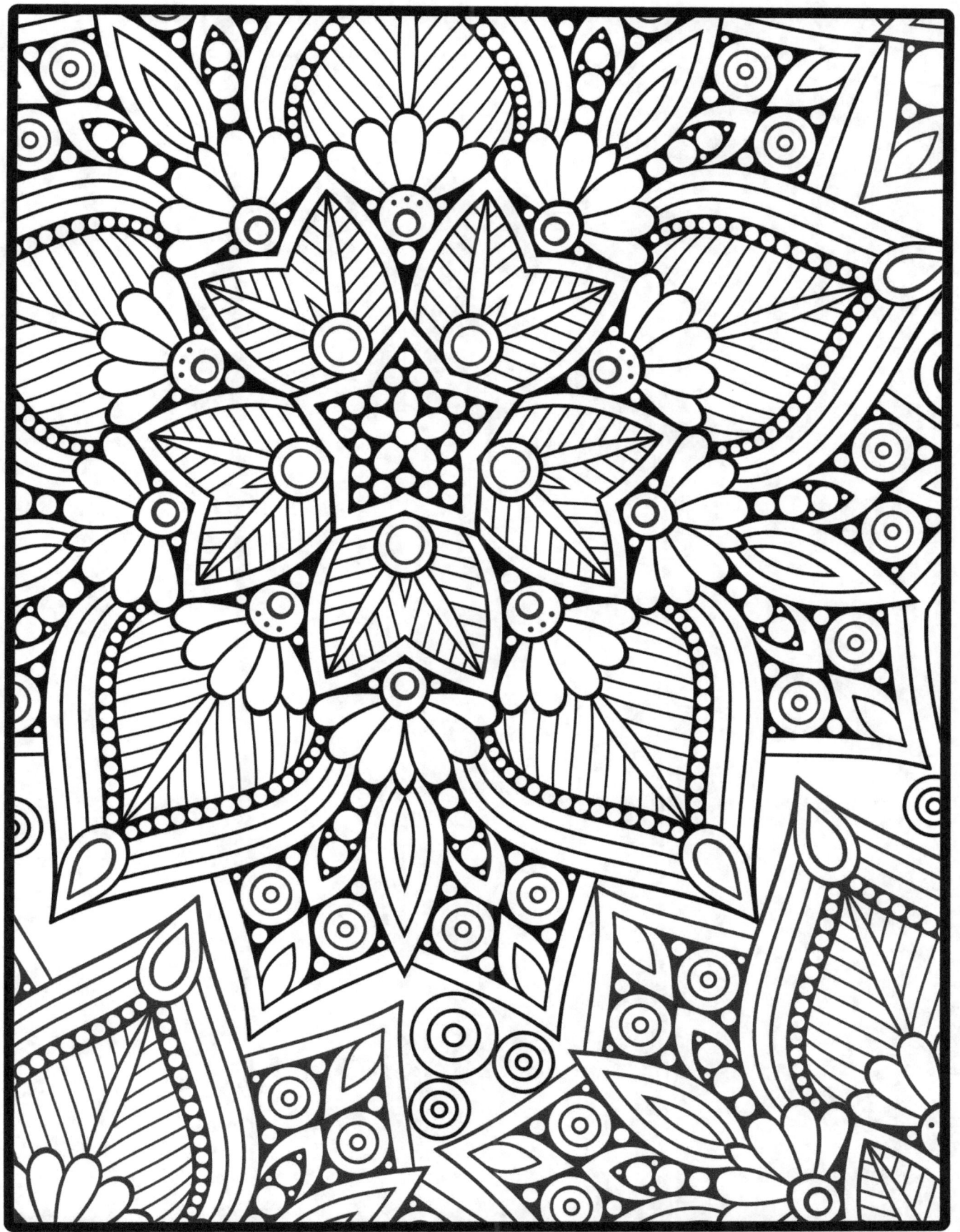

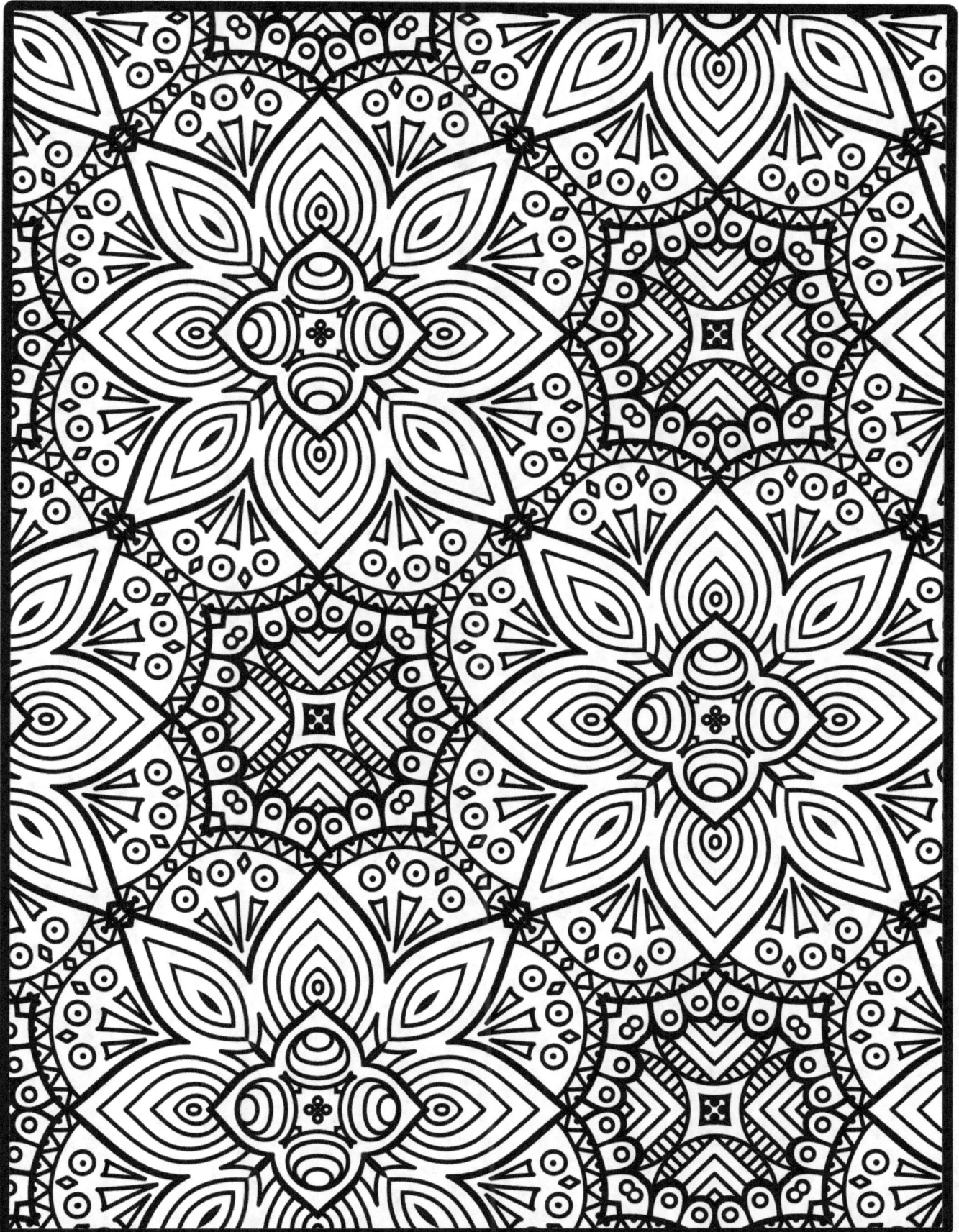

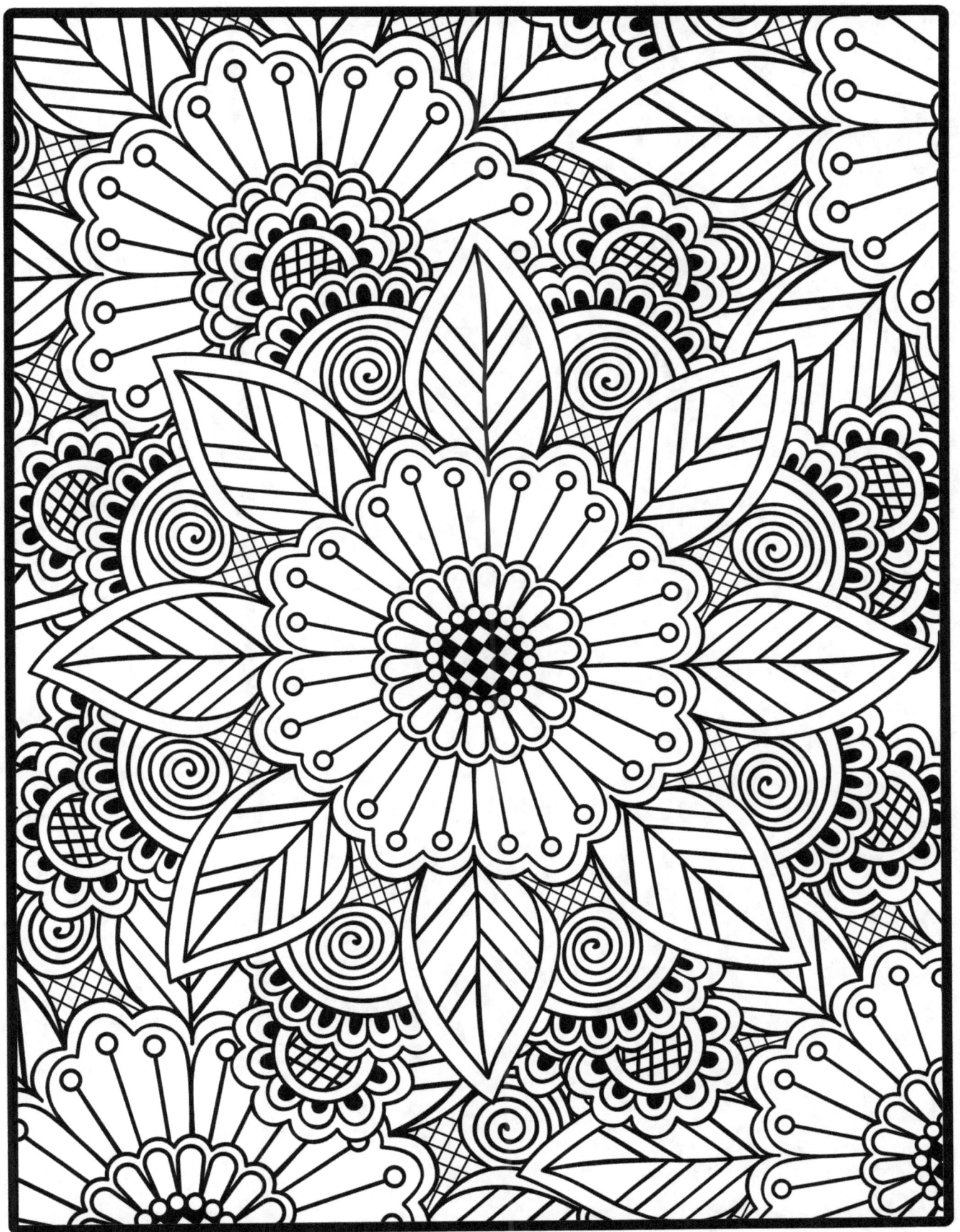

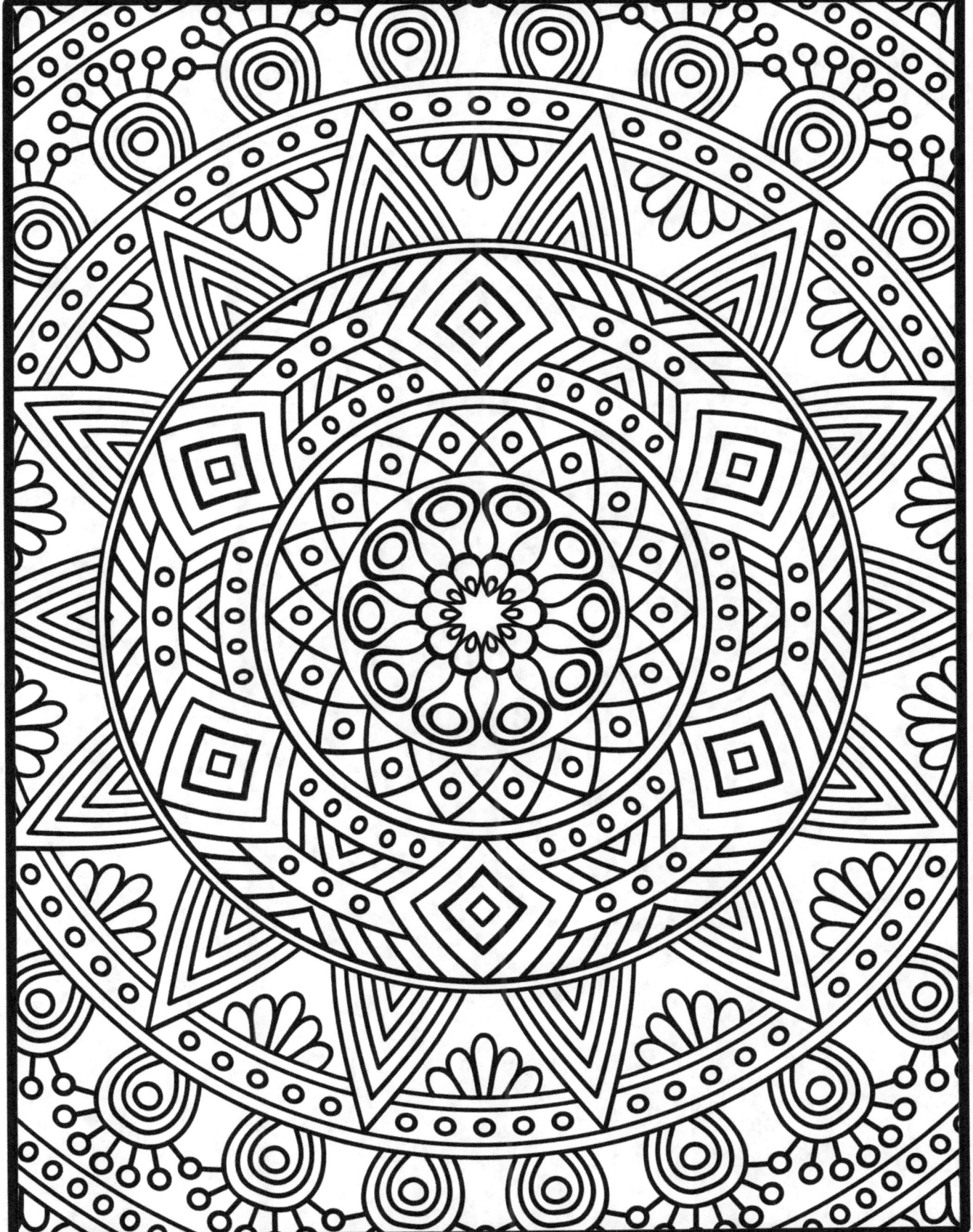

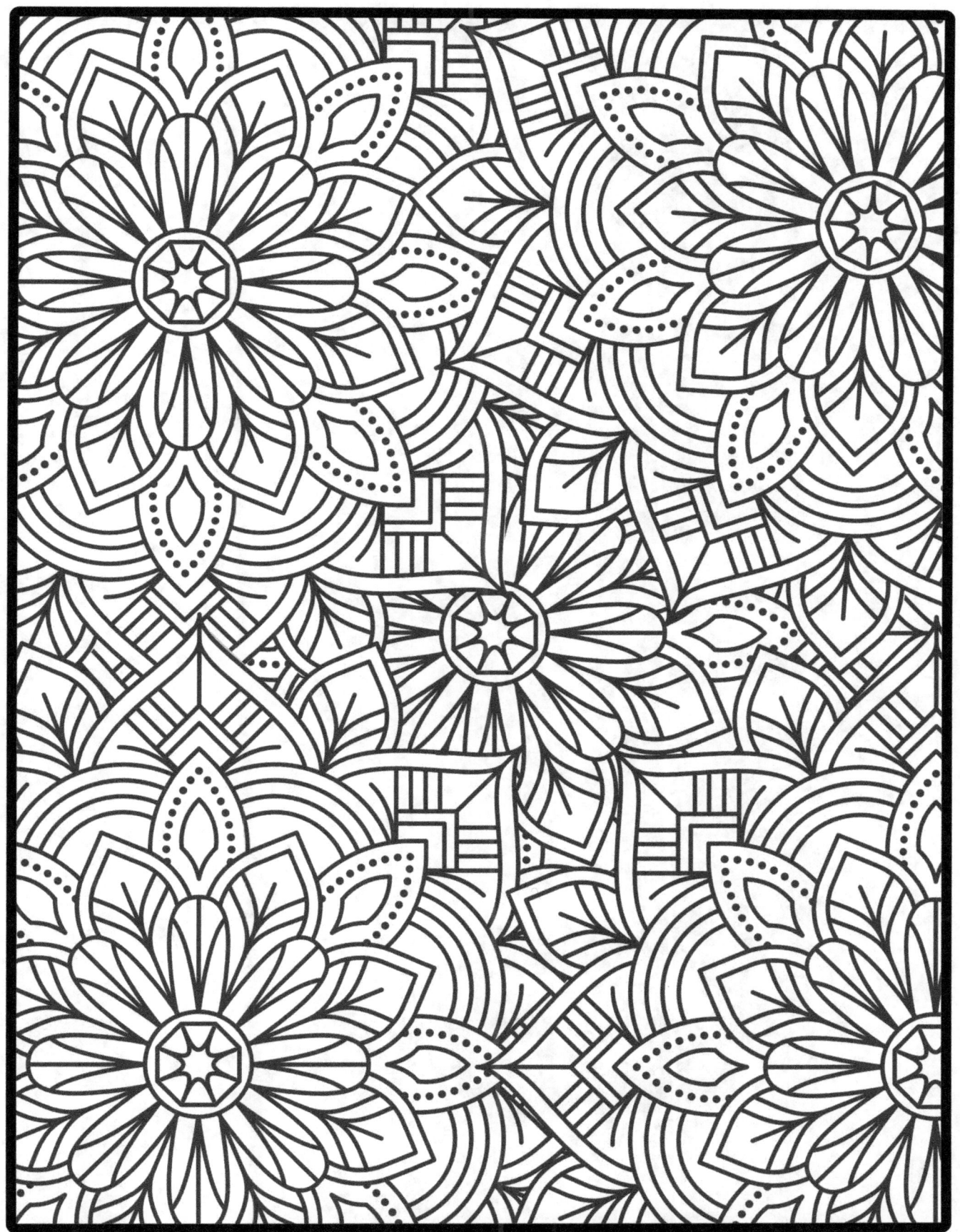

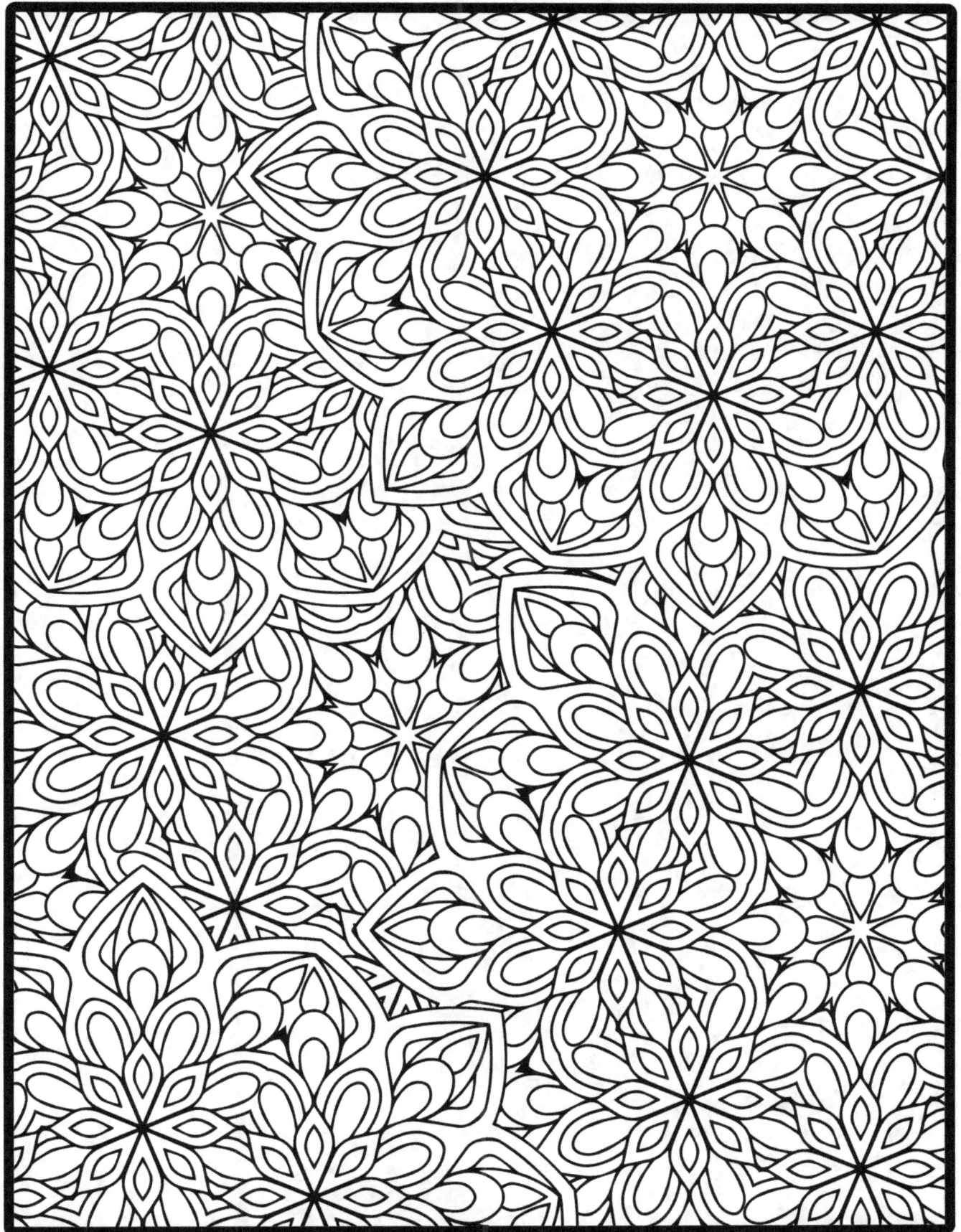

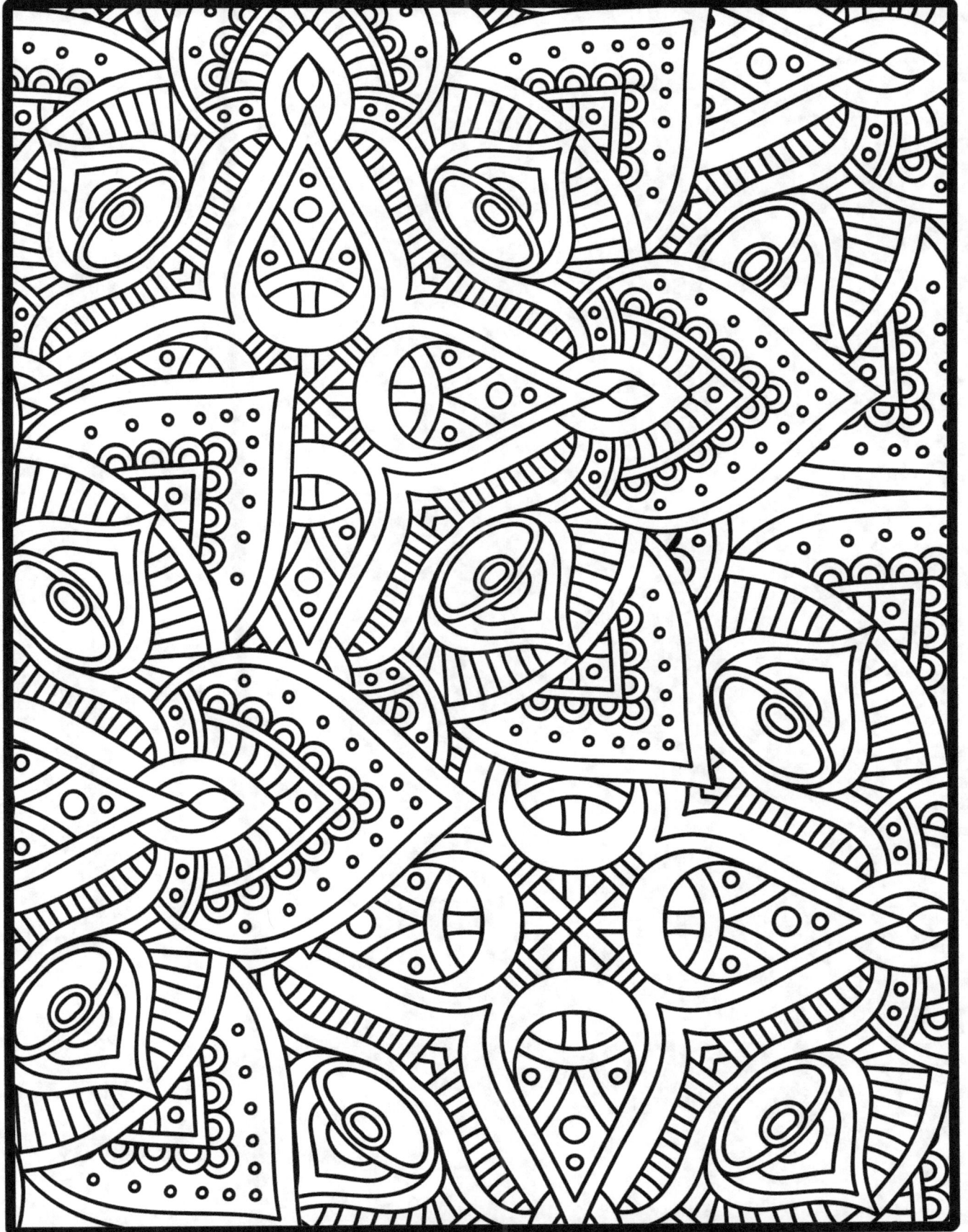

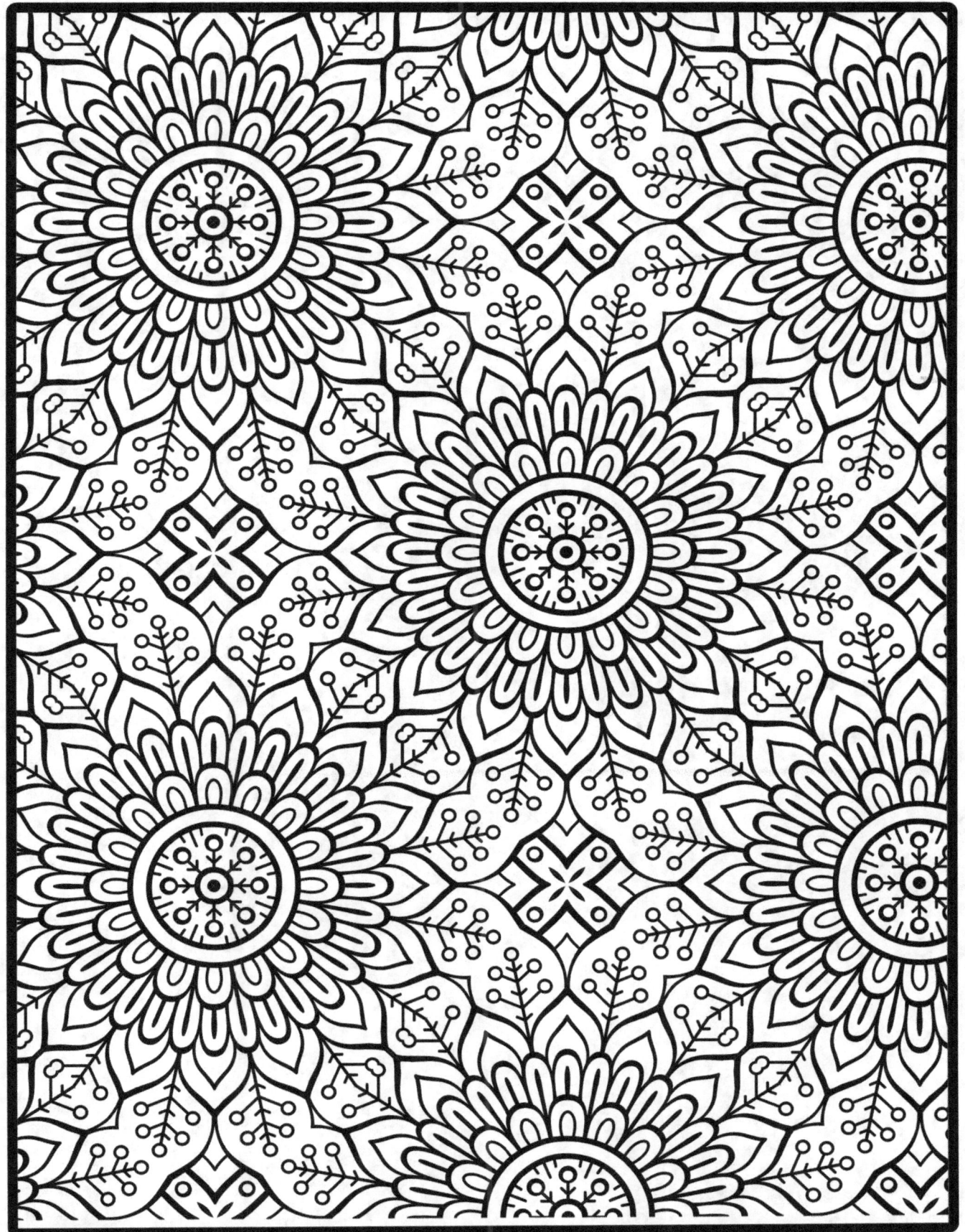

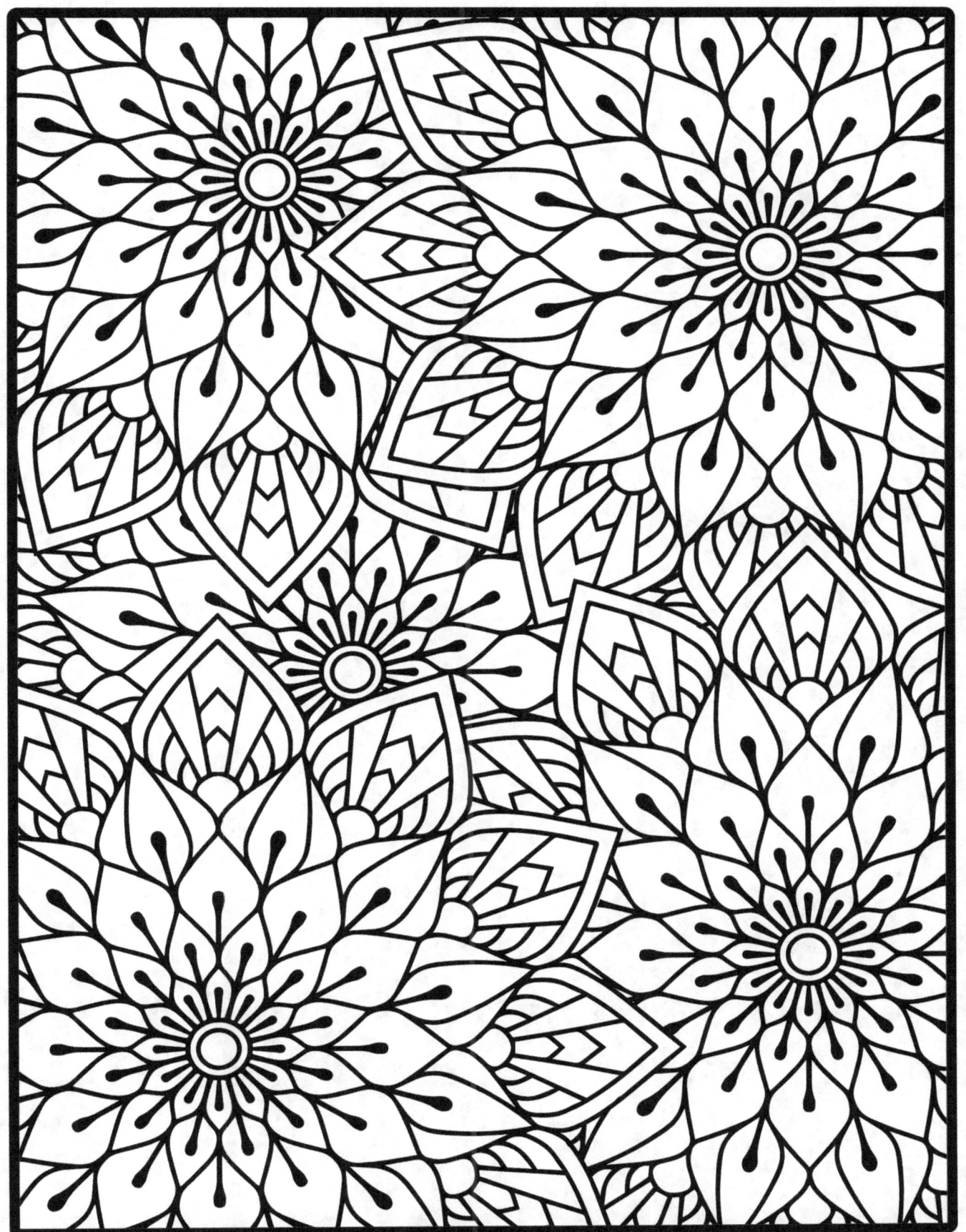

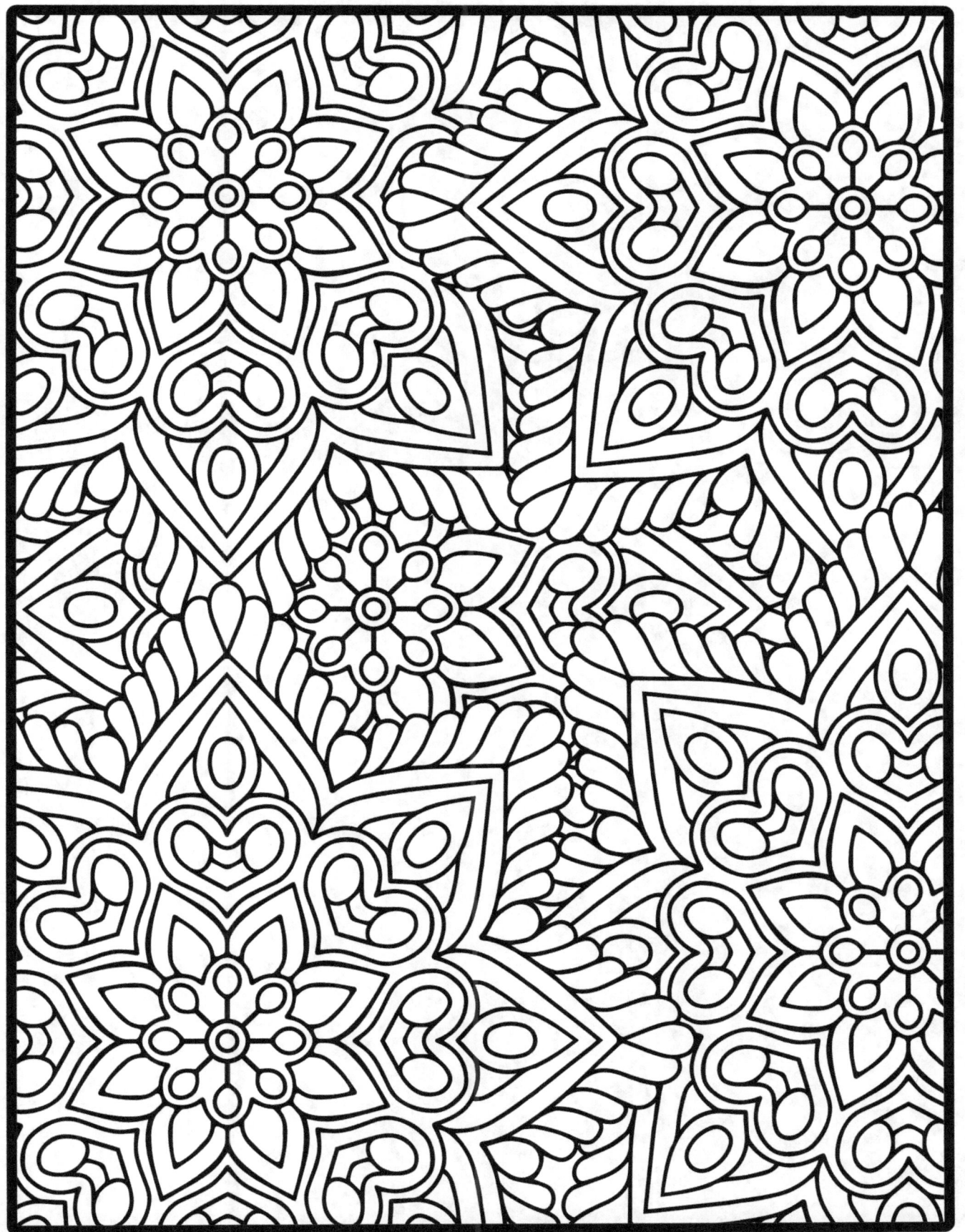

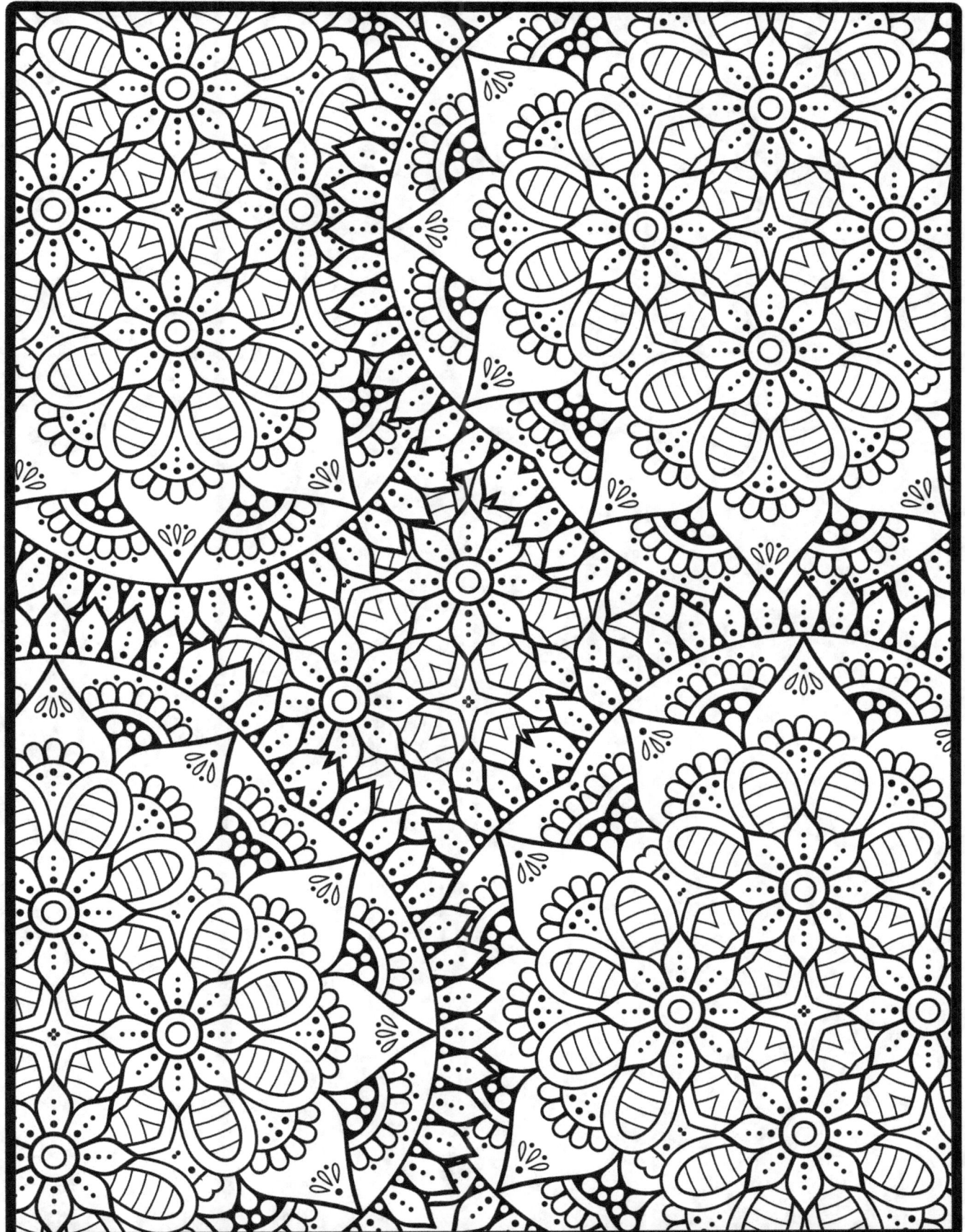

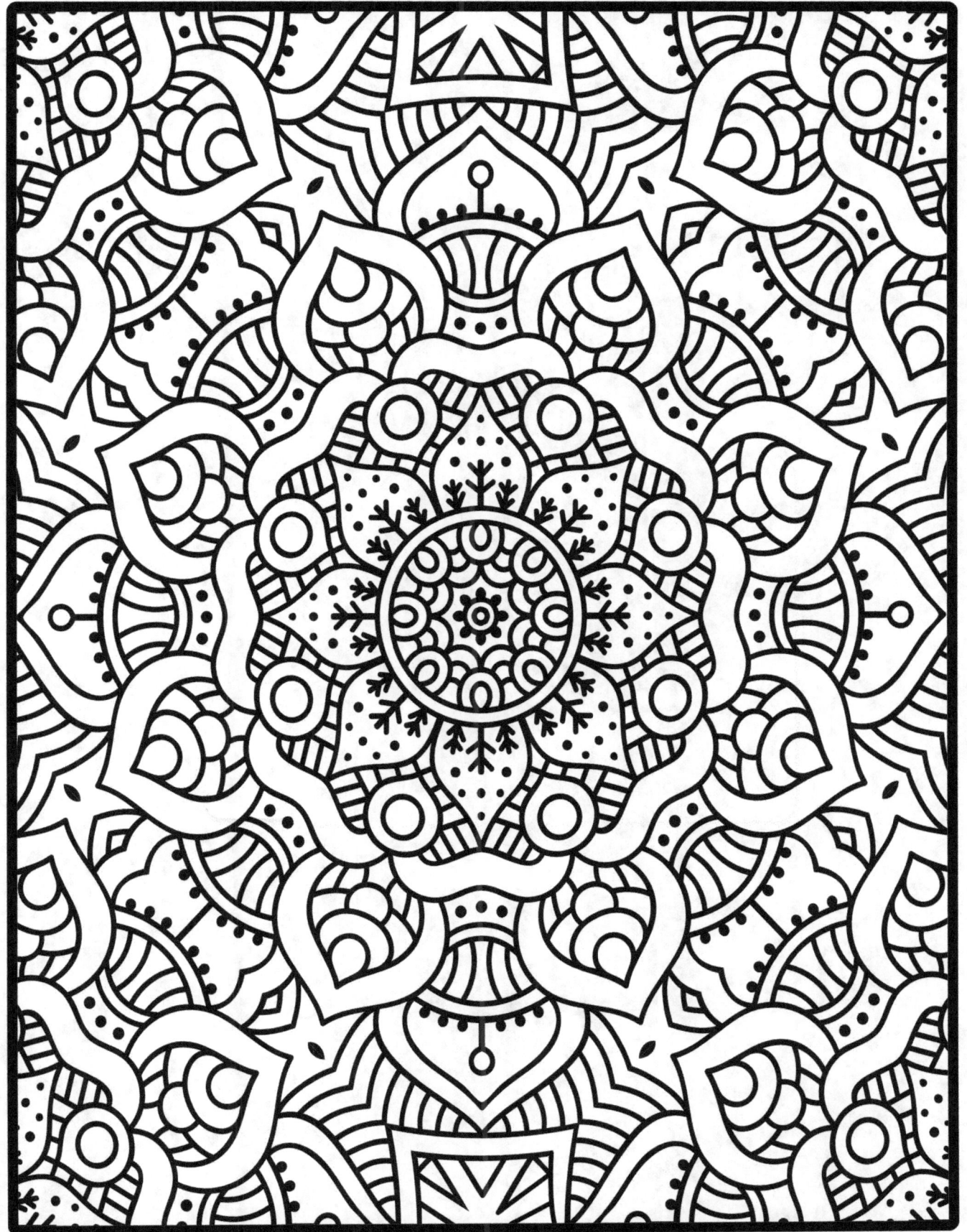

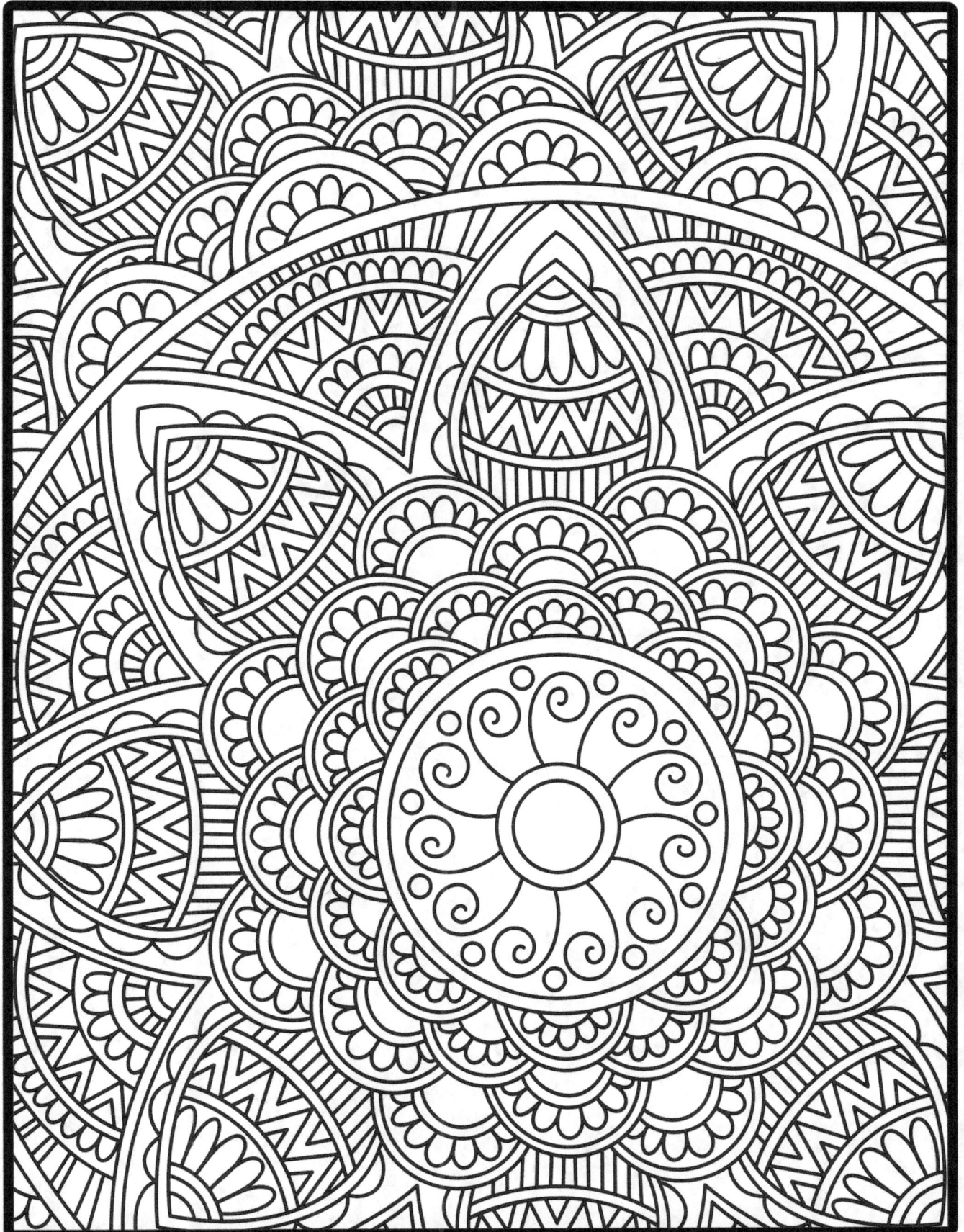

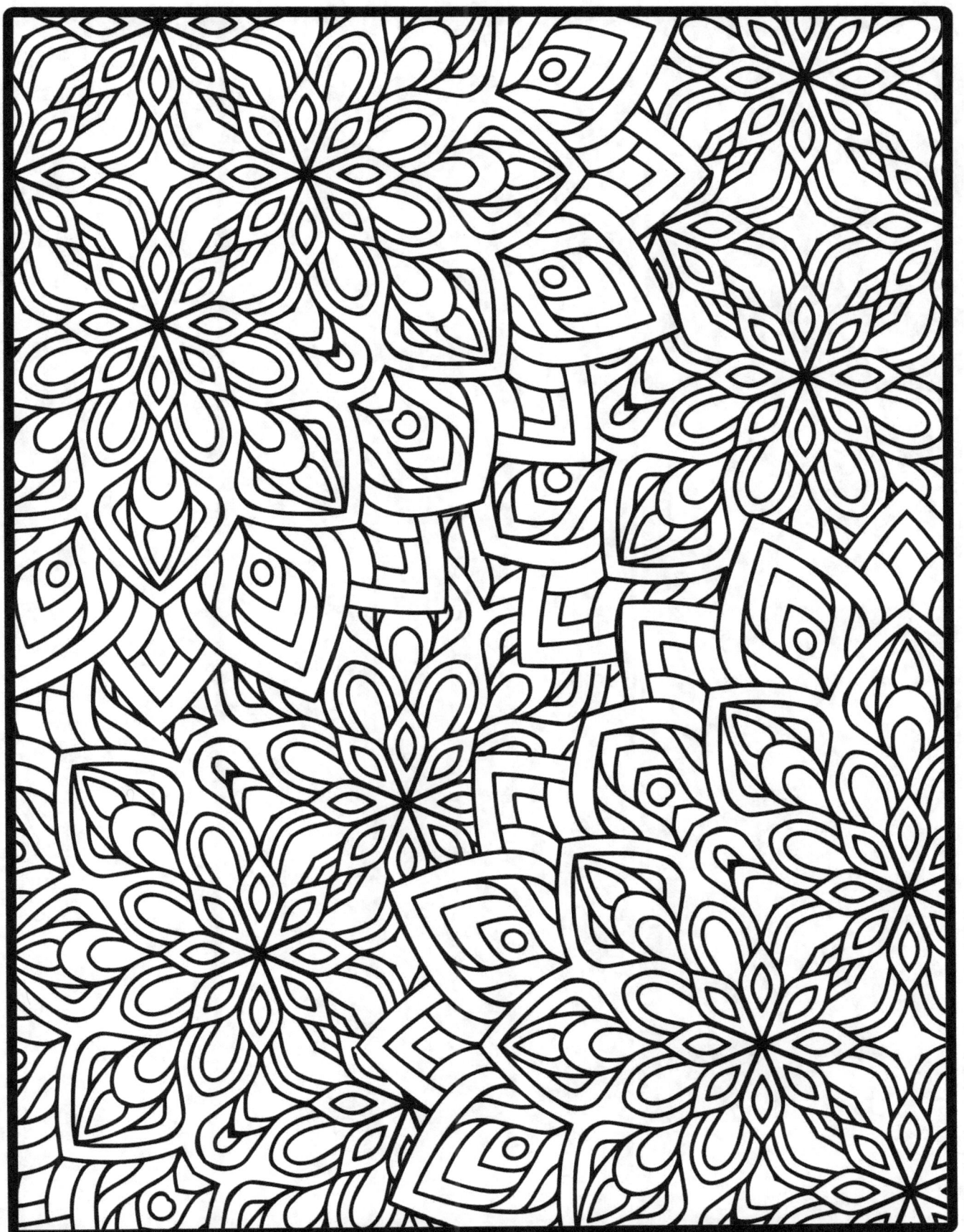

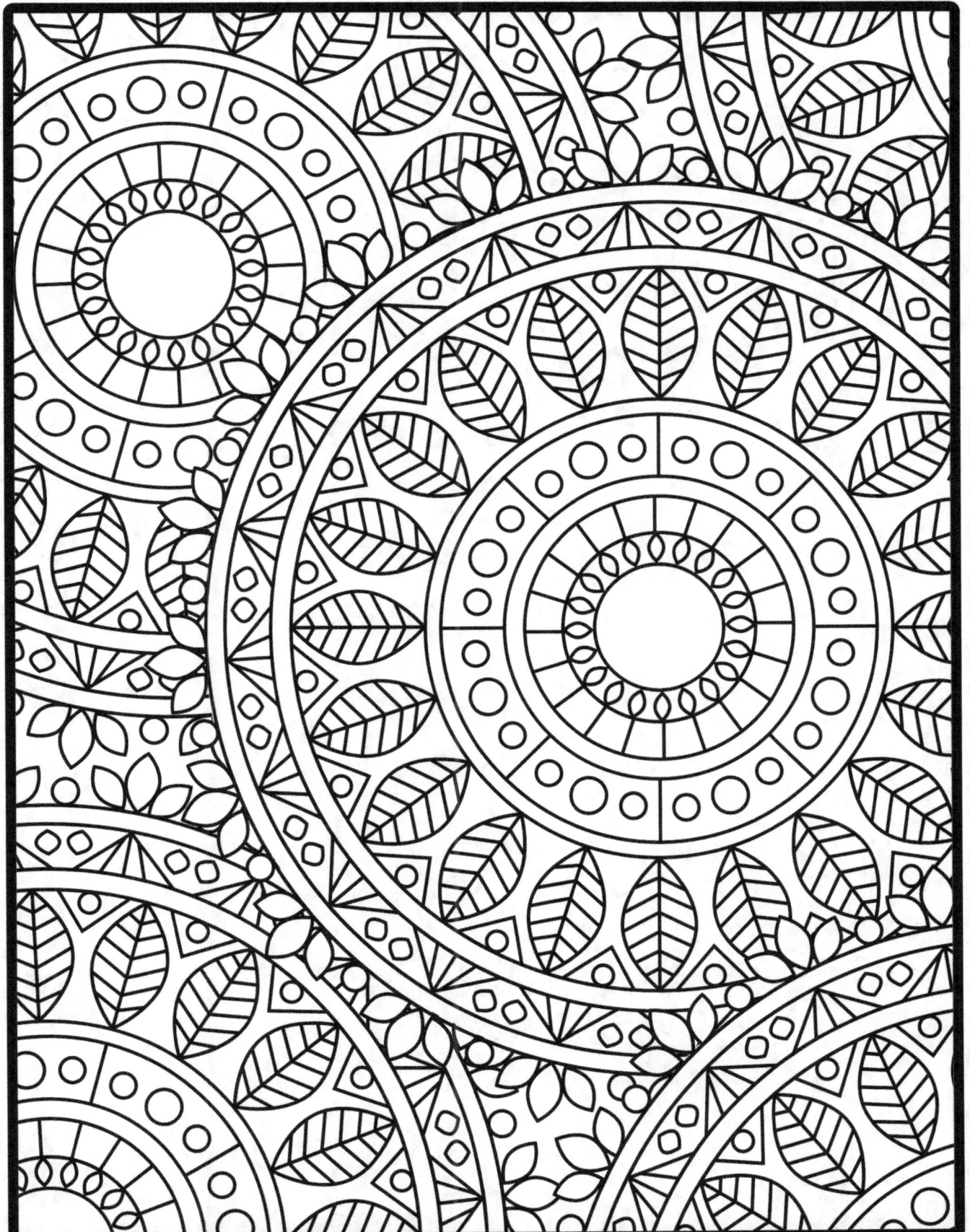

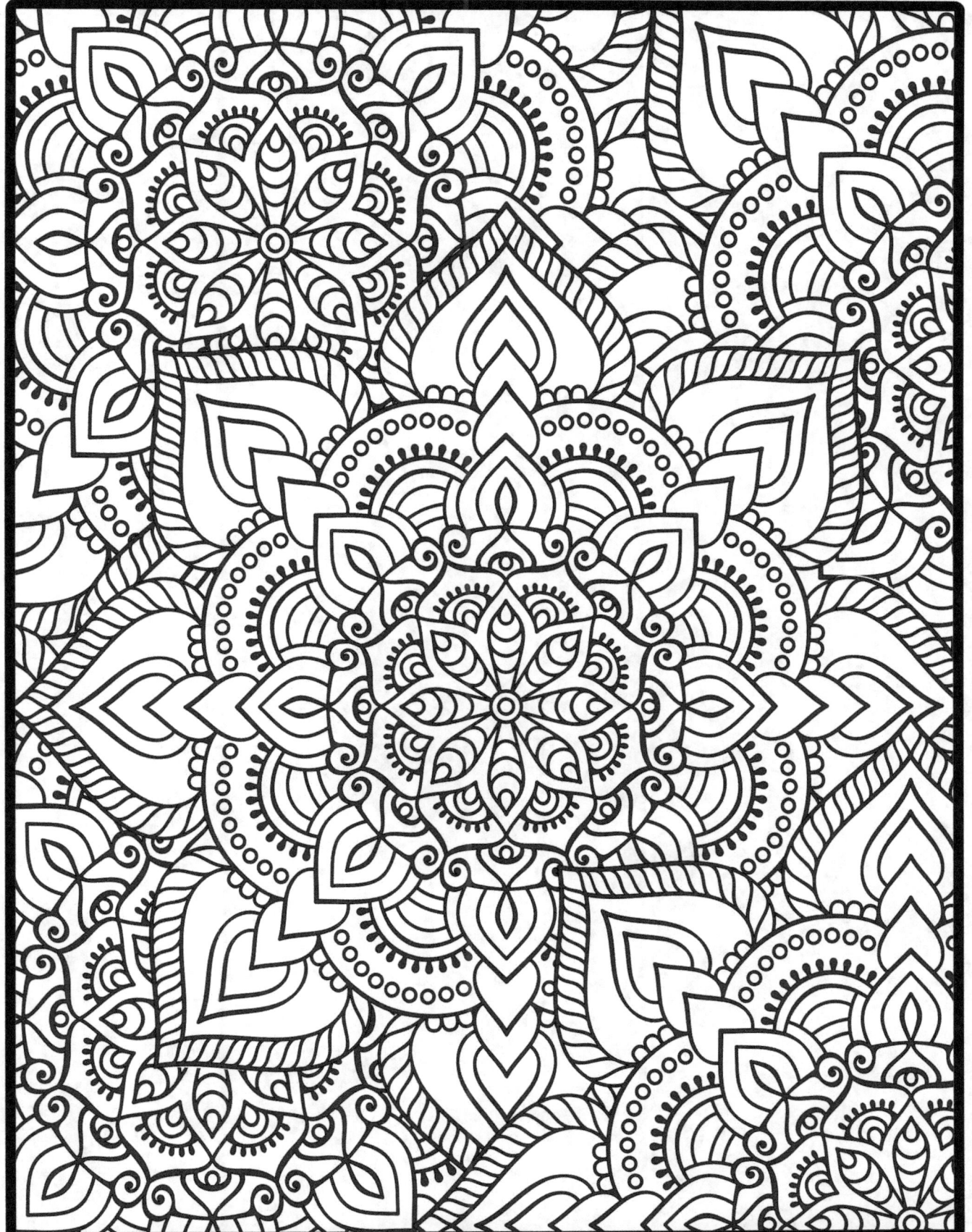

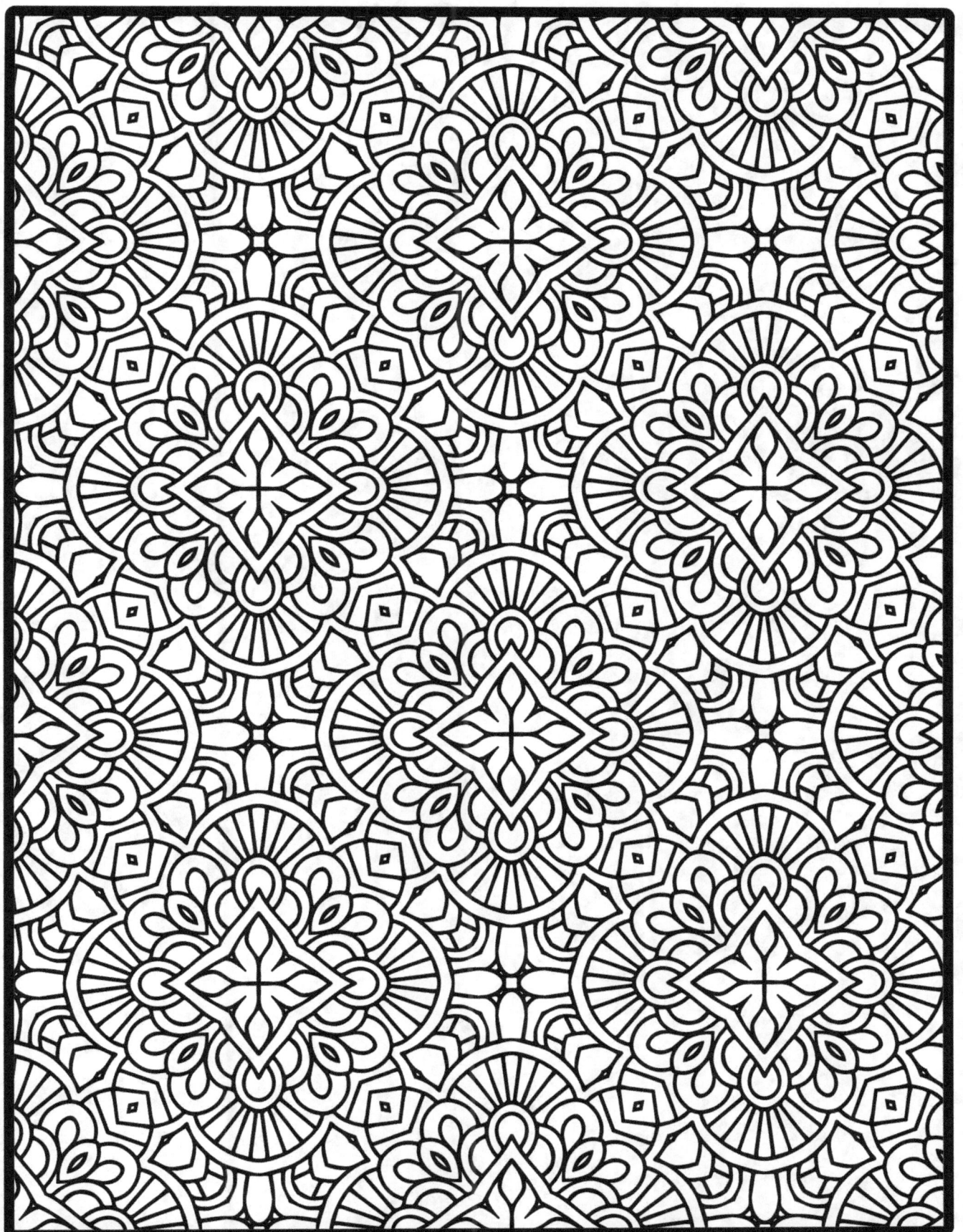

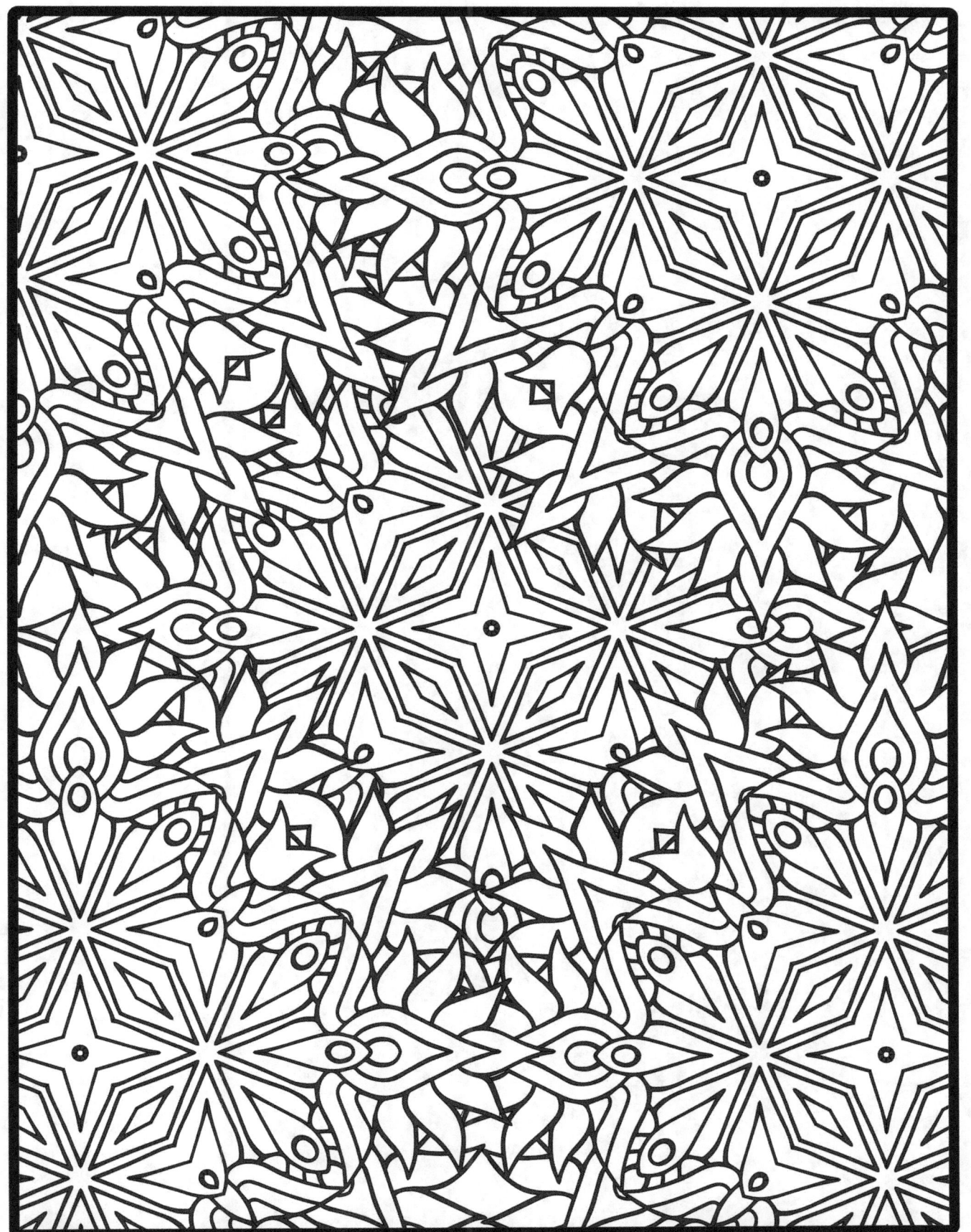

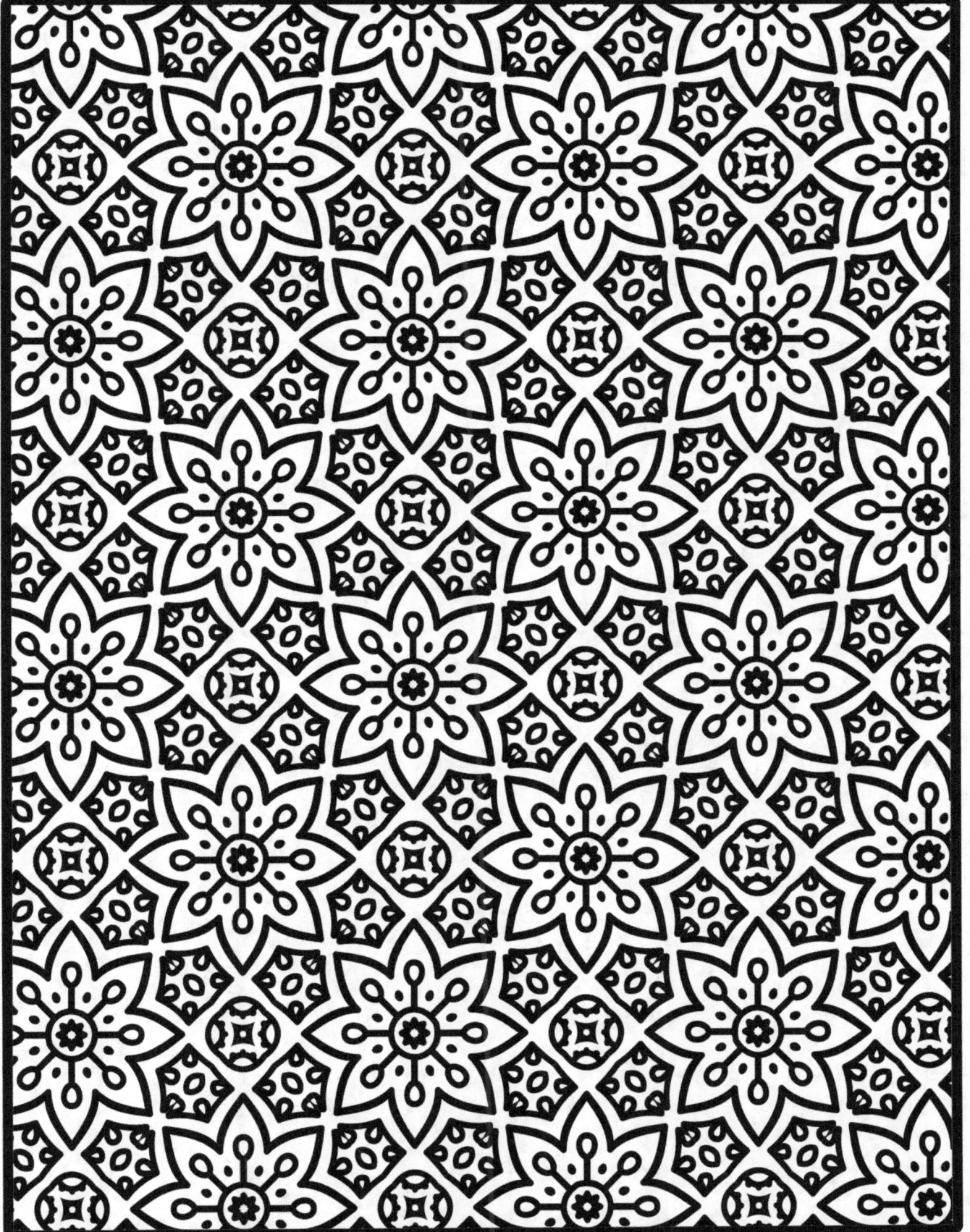

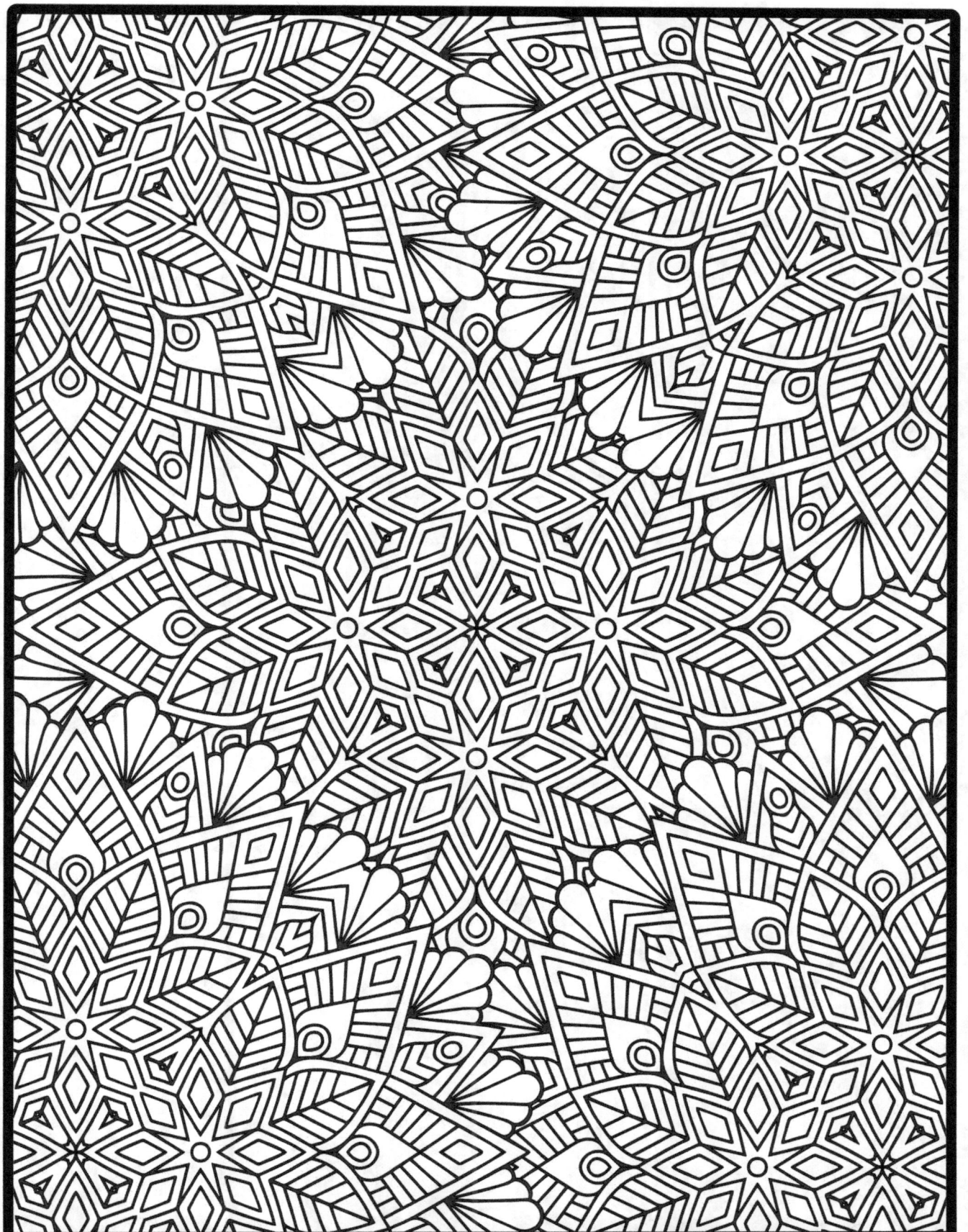

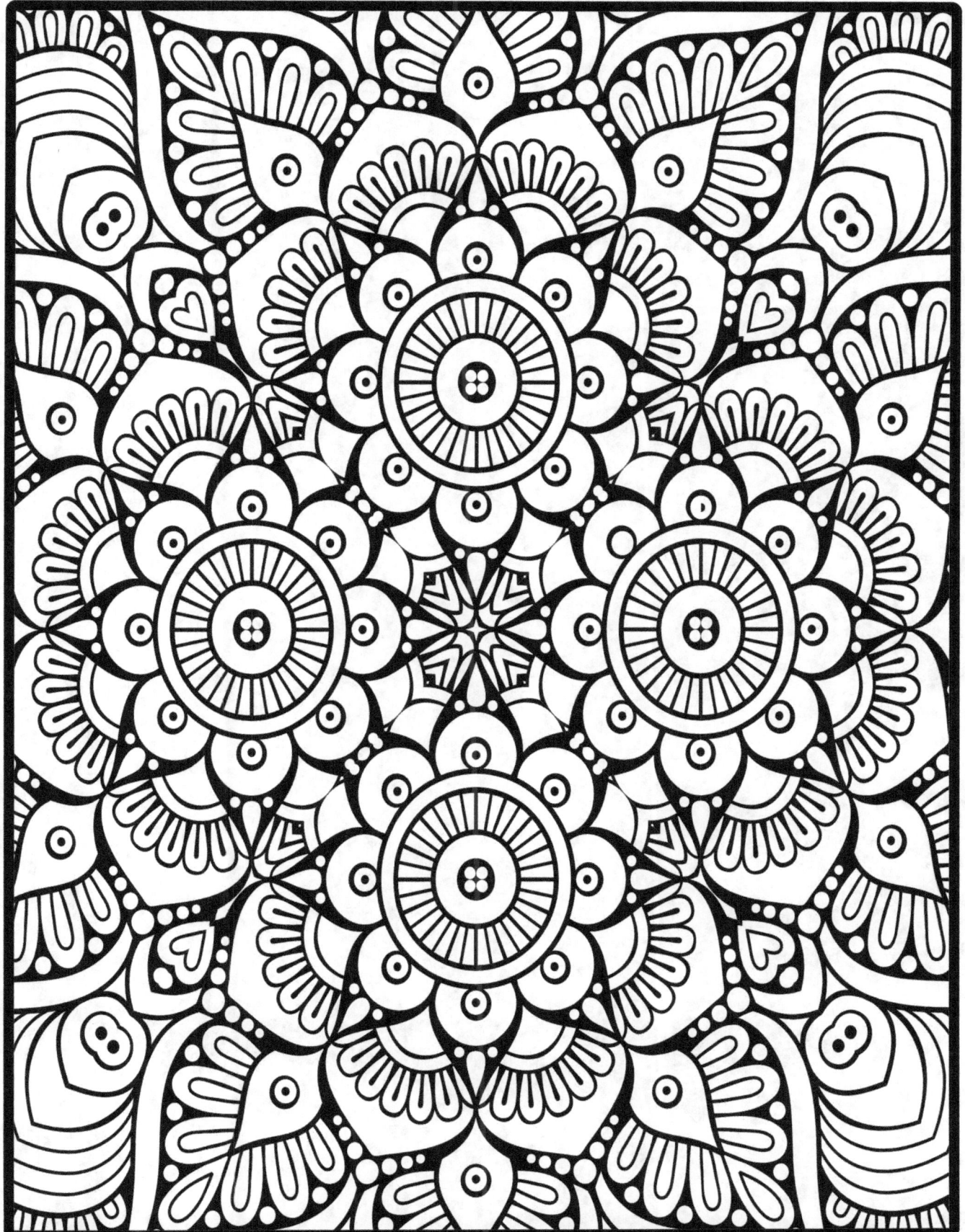

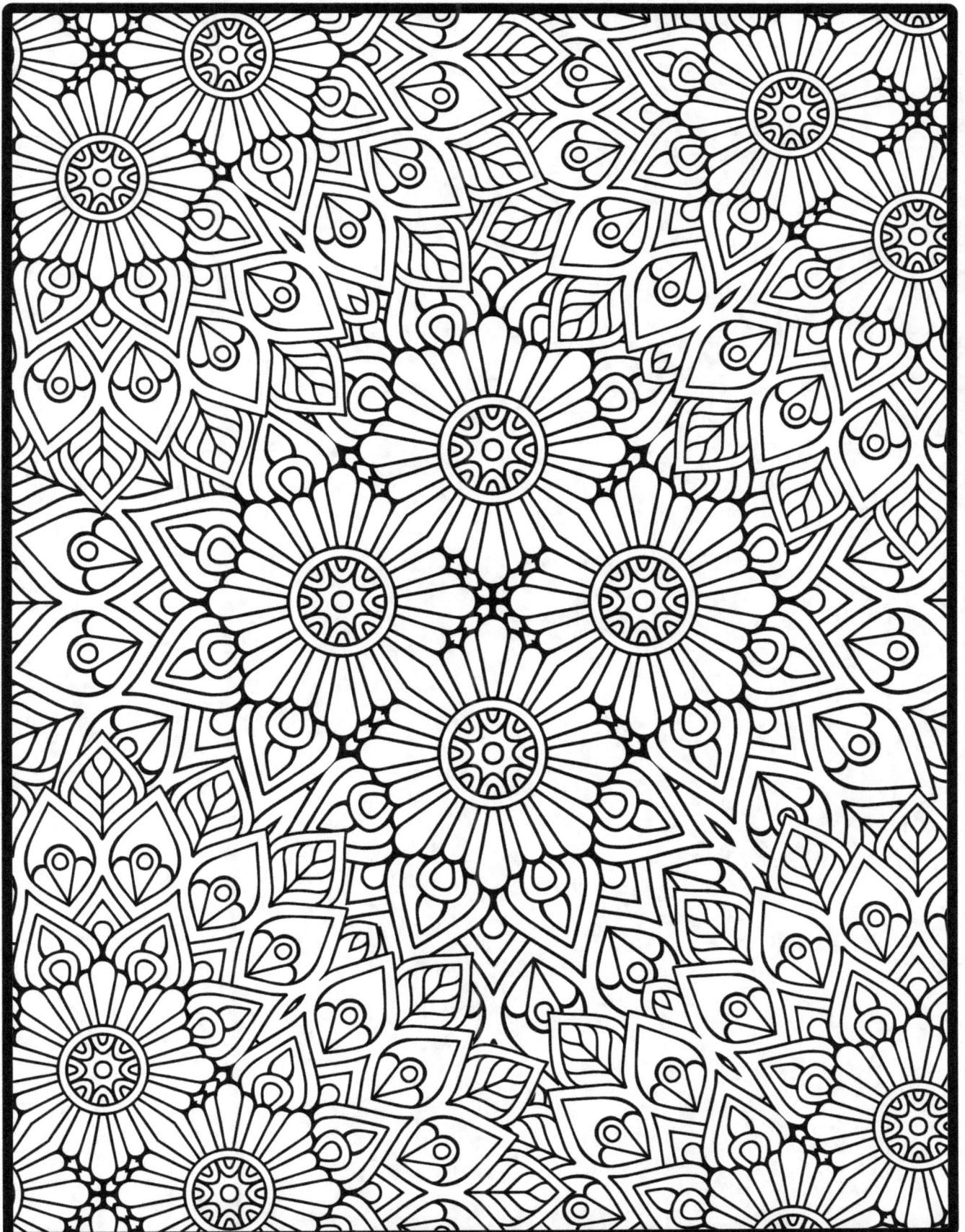

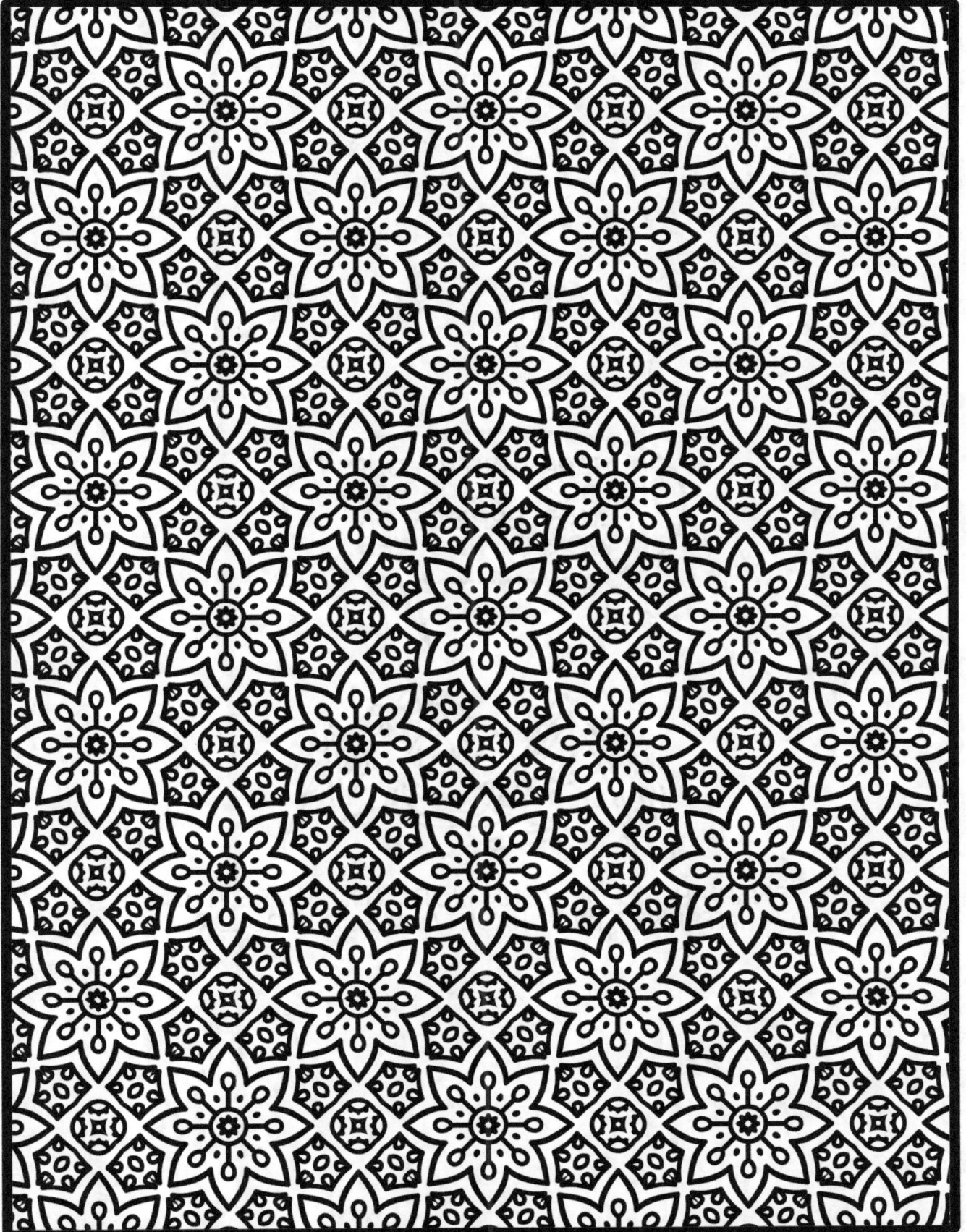

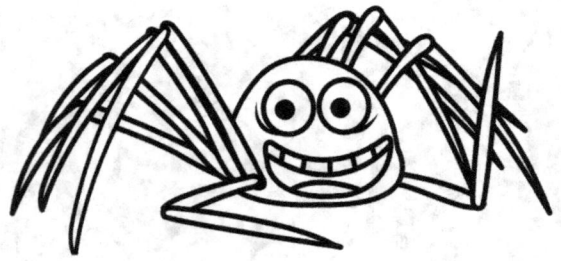

SNAP PHOTO OF YOUR WORK AND SHARE IT ON INTERNET WITH HASHTAG #SOPHIACOLOR

www.ingramcontent.com/pod-product-compliance
Lightning Source LLC
Chambersburg PA
CBHW080617220526
45466CB00010B/3365